Almost Perfect

Jerry Mayer

A Samuel French Acting Edition

FOUNDED 1830

SAMUELFRENCH.COM
SAMUELFRENCH-LONDON.CO.UK

Copyright © 1988, 1989 by Jerry Mayer
All Rights Reserved

ALMOST PERFECT is fully protected under the copyright laws of the United States of America, the British Commonwealth, including Canada, and all other countries of the Copyright Union. All rights, including professional and amateur stage productions, recitation, lecturing, public reading, motion picture, radio broadcasting, television and the rights of translation into foreign languages are strictly reserved.

ISBN 978-0-573-69095-2

www.SamuelFrench.com
www.SamuelFrench-London.co.uk

For Production Enquiries

United States and Canada
Info@SamuelFrench.com
1-866-598-8449

United Kingdom and Europe
Plays@SamuelFrench-London.co.uk
020-7255-4302

Each title is subject to availability from Samuel French, depending upon country of performance. Please be aware that *ALMOST PERFECT* may not be licensed by Samuel French in your territory. Professional and amateur producers should contact the nearest Samuel French office or licensing partner to verify availability.

CAUTION: Professional and amateur producers are hereby warned that *ALMOST PERFECT* is subject to a licensing fee. Publication of this play(s) does not imply availability for performance. Both amateurs and professionals considering a production are strongly advised to apply to Samuel French before starting rehearsals, advertising, or booking a theatre. A licensing fee must be paid whether the title(s) is presented for charity or gain and whether or not admission is charged. Professional/Stock licensing fees are quoted upon application to Samuel French.

No one shall make any changes in this title(s) for the purpose of production. No part of this book may be reproduced, stored in a retrieval system, or transmitted in any form, by any means, now known or yet to be invented, including mechanical, electronic, photocopying, recording, videotaping, or otherwise, without the prior written permission of the publisher. No one shall upload this title(s), or part of this title(s), to any social media websites.

For all enquiries regarding motion picture, television, and other media rights, please contact Samuel French.

MUSIC USE NOTE

Licensees are solely responsible for obtaining formal written permission from copyright owners to use copyrighted music in the performance of this play and are strongly cautioned to do so. If no such permission is obtained by the licensee, then the licensee must use only original music that the licensee owns and controls. Licensees are solely responsible and liable for all music clearances and shall indemnify the copyright owners of the play(s) and their licensing agent, Samuel French, against any costs, expenses, losses and liabilities arising from the use of music by licensees. Please contact the appropriate music licensing authority in your territory for the rights to any incidental music.

IMPORTANT BILLING AND CREDIT REQUIREMENTS

If you have obtained performance rights to this title, please refer to your licensing agreement for important billing and credit requirements.

FOR MOM AND DAD
AND FOR EMILY

ALMOST PERFECT was originally presented at Santa Monica Playhouse (Chris DeCarlo and Evelyn Rudie, Artistic Directors) in Santa Monica, Ca, produced by Emily Bettman Mayer and Santa Monica Playhouse, on August 14th, 1986. It was directed by Martin M. Speer; the set design was by Scott Heineman; the lighting was by Matthew O'Donnell; the sound was by Evelyn Rudie and the production stage manager was Russell Werthman. The cast, in order of appearance, was as follows:

BUDDY .... Charles Levin
JENNY............................... Alley Mills
DAD .... Norman Burton*
MIKE .... Todd Susman
BOOTS .... Sandra Kerns
MOM .... Naomi Serotoff

*This part was originally cast and was subsequently played by Bruce Kirby.

A different production of ALMOST PERFECT was presented at the Hudson Guild Theatre (Geoffrey Sherman, Producing Director) in New York City, produced by the Hudson Guild Theatre, in association with Emily Bettman Mayer, on November 30th, 1988. It was directed by Geraldine Fitzgerald; the set design was by James D. Sandefur; the lighting was by Phil Monat; the costumes were by Pamela Scofield; the sound was by Aural Fixation; and the production stage manager was Frederick Hahn. The cast, in order of appearance, was as follows:

BUDDY .... Ethan Phillips
JENNY................................ Mia Dillon
DAD .... Bill Nelson
MIKE .... Ivar Brogger
BOOTS .... Cathy Lee Crosby
MOM............................... Chevi Colton

TIME

The present, during June, July and August.

PLACE

St. Louis, Mo.

ACT I

The action takes place at different locations in St. Louis.

ACT II

Six weeks later.

(Scenes flow continuously, without stopping.)

CAST OF CHARACTERS

BUDDY APPLE
Early to mid thirties. Sexy, but not handsome. There's an intensity about Buddy, an inner urgency, perhaps from a constant struggle between doing what's "right" and doing what's right for him. Buddy is a nice guy but not a goody goody or a wimp. He possesses that selfishness of survival that's in all of us. His irreverent sense of humor helps him deal with the daily frustrations caused by his father and his wife.

JENNY APPLE
Buddy's wife. Early thirties. She is slim and attractive, but noticably understated. Jenny is a "good citizen," responsible, organized, honest and frugal. She's the anchor for her family. She is not mousy or a drudge. She has a wonderful spirit, a sense of humor and a great laugh. During Act II, Jenny goes through a metamorphasis, blossoming, both in appearance and emotion.

DAD APPLE
Buddy's father. Sixtyish, the boss of Apple Construction, a totally self-made man, the ultimate energetic super-salesman. He's charming and impish, yet forceful and manipulative.

MIKE APPLE
Buddy's older brother, late thirties. Attractive, virile, sure of himself. A man of definite opinions, especially about women. You might call him crude, but it wouldn't bother him.

Characters
(continued)

BOOTS CLARK
That unattainable dream of perfection. Boots, in her thirties, has it all: beauty, breeding, wit, intelligence, sensitivity and success.

MOM APPLE
Sixtyish, a few years younger than Dad. Attractive, non-demanding and even tempered. She's happy, as long as her husband and sons are getting along.

(DAD Enters, crosses to BUDDY with a sign: "APPLE CONSTRUCTION PRESENTS ... MADONNA LAKES ESTATES." A moment after DAD Enters, MIKE Exits.)

DAD. Well, here it is, Madonna Lakes Estates. Whataya think, kiddo?

BUDDY. You know what I think. What do you want to name the models. "The Father," "The Son," and "The Holy Ghost?"

DAD. Funny, we'll name them after lakes. The Como, The Lugano, The Geneva ... *(He puts the new sign over "Heather Highlands.")*

BUDDY. "The Titticaca?" Dad, we all three agreed on "Heather Highlands."

DAD. I know, but my stomach didn't agree.

BUDDY. *(complaining to the audience)* His *stomach.* The fourth member of the firm.

DAD. Last night, at two in the morning, it was saying, "Heather Highlands? That sounds so 'tippy toe.' We're selling to Italians not ballet dancers. Italians are Catholic, so why go Scottish?"

BUDDY. You loved Scottish. It says value.

DAD. It also says cheap. Why remind people they're poor? It pisses them off. "Madonna Lakes Estates" will sell houses.

BUDDY. Dad, how can you call two bedrooms, one bath, on a thirty foot lot, an estate?

DAD. Every man's home is his estate. My pal, my goombah, Bishop Balducci at the Archdiocese, suggested the name, "Madonna." And the Catholic Church knows real estate. They own most of St. Louis tax free. So,

BUDDY. Oops, almost forgot. The obligatory kiss. Just kidding. *(He kisses her.)* Let it ring awhile. It makes him crazy. *(BUDDY Exits. JENNY picks up the phone.)*

JENNY. *(into the phone)* Hello? Oh, hi, Dad. — No, he hasn't called. Dad, you're planning to vote today, aren't you? There are a lot of important measures on the ballot. — Good. Get a pencil.

(LIGHTS out on JENNY. LIGHTS up on BUDDY. As he talks in limbo, we hear an interlude of our MUSIC.)

BUDDY. *(to the audience:)* Just another average day, working for my father. *Undoing* everything that I worked my ass off *doing,* yesterday.

(LIGHTS up on the sales office, consisting of a couch and a chair and table. We see a sign, hanging or on a tripod. "APPLE CONSTRUCTION PRESENTS HEATHER HIGHLANDS." MIKE APPLE [37], in jeans, boots and plaid shirt, is moving furniture into place.)

MIKE. Buddy, where you been all day?

BUDDY. Putting a hold on Heather Highlands brochures, Heather Highlands billboards and three hundred and fifty yards of plaid carpeting. Where's Dad?

MIKE. All over the fuckin' place. He's bringing in the new sign.

BUDDY. Goddamit. You couldn't talk him out of it?

MIKE. Did you ever try taking meat from a pit bull?

would do. *(DAD Exits.)*

BUDDY. *(to the audience:)* Of *course* I bought the engagement ring. Of *course* I went into the building business. If Gershwin had a father like mine, he wouldn't have written *chopsticks.*

(JENNY Enters. BUDDY tosses the letter sweater over his shoulder. She catches it, puts it away.)

BUDDY. I swear to God, if he insists on "Madonna Lakes Estates," I'm quitting. *(He puts on an Ivy League sportcoat and a rep tie. She finishes getting dressed.)*

JENNY. You're not quitting. You can't afford to lose that job.

BUDDY. Why not? I sold two cartoons to Playboy last month. And my screenplay is getting better all the time.

JENNY. Buddy, you're not ready to earn a living in Hollywood yet. You earned a total of four hundred and sixty five dollars last year, selling your jokes and cartoons.

BUDDY. Nothing like getting support from your wife.

JENNY. Will you grow up! We have responsibilities, we have expenses. When you make a million dollars, then you can be a writer.

(The TELEPHONE rings. BUDDY reacts.)

BUDDY. That's Dad again. I've already left.
JENNY. Wait! *(She purses her lips for a kiss.)*

ought to protect your interest with a little commitment.

BUDDY. Commitment? Dad, I'm only twenty two, I want to wait a while.

DAD. Buddy, good deals get away when you wait. Son, when you find a good deal, that's lucky. When you *know* it's a good deal, that's smart. And getting the person you're gonna live your life with is the most important deal there is.

BUDDY. Are you talking about marriage?

DAD. Marriage? Are you crazy? I'm talking about an engagement ring, to tie her up. Like an earnest money contract. I know, you're worried about the cost.

BUDDY. I wasn't worried about a thing.

DAD. Buddy, you were a great carpenter's apprentice last summer. As far as I'm concerned, you've got a permanent job, inside the office, with Mike and me.

BUDDY. Thanks, Dad, but I'm not sure I want to stay in the building business. I want to give writing a try.

DAD. You mean your jokes? You can do that, too. In the meantime, you've got to live. I just want you to know, *if* you should decide on a ring, I'll advance you the money. Y'know, against your wedding present.

BUDDY. Wedding present?

DAD. Yeah, you'll get ten thousand, just like Mom and I gave Mike.

BUDDY. Ten thousand?

DAD. And I'm not gonna let you work for slave wages if you're engaged. I plan to double your salary.

BUDDY. *(impressed)* Jesus, Dad.

DAD. *But ... it's your decision.* I know what smart money

waste a whole summer?" So he bought me a hammer and gave me a job. Gershwin had a wonderful father. He bought George a piano and left him alone.

(LIGHTS come up on NORMAN APPLE [DAD], in limbo, wearing a sleeveless sweater, reading some blueprints.)

DAD. Buddy, where you going? You're not even home for meals anymore. Let's have a little talk.

BUDDY. Dad, I've got a date with Jenny and I'm late already.

DAD. *That's* what I want to talk about. You know how Mom and I feel about Jenny. Great girl, fine Jewish family.

BUDDY. Yeah, you've mentioned that.

DAD. Mom just told me Jenny's transferring to Northwestern.

BUDDY. That's right.

DAD. Between us girls, wouldn't you rather keep her here in St. Louis?

BUDDY. Dad, it's Jenny's decision and it's where she wants to...

DAD. *(Interrupts, squeezing BUDDY'S cheeks.)* Good, don't forget what you wanted to say. Jenny could meet all kinds of football heroes and fraternity boys at Northwestern. Three hundred miles away, in a coed dorm.

BUDDY. That won't matter. We have an understanding.

DAD. And I have a septic tank, and they're both full of good intentions. Buddy, you've got a face your mother could never forget. But your girlfriend *might*. Maybe you

(The TELEPHONE rings.)

BUDDY. Oh no, I'll bet that's Dad. Tell him I'm gone.

JENNY. I can't lie to your father.

BUDDY. Sure you can. Try it, it's fun. He believes anything you say. *Please?*

JENNY. *(She picks up the phone.)* Hello? Oh, hi, Dad. — Sorry, you just missed him. — Gee, I'm not sure if he was going to the printer's or not. Okay, Dad. Yeah, see you at dinner tonight. Goodbye. *(She hangs up the phone.)*

BUDDY. Goddammit!

JENNY. I thought I was a wonderful liar.

BUDDY. Not you, *Dad.* I'll bet he wants to stop the brochures. He's not sure he likes the name "Heather Highlands" anymore for our new building project.

JENNY. But he loved that name when you came up with it.

BUDDY. That's before he thought of a better name, that'll really appeal to the Italians on the South side. "Madonna Lakes Estates."

JENNY. But there aren't any lakes.

BUDDY. There will be. *(to the audience:)* Give my father a bulldozer and a garden hose and he becomes God.

(JENNY Exits. BUDDY puts on a high school letter sweater to suggest a flashback. We hear MUSIC under the following.)

BUDDY. Nothing's changed. When I graduated high school, I wanted to hitchhike to Hollywood one summer. I could've made great contacts out there. Dad said, "Why

BUDDY. But it's not what I wanted! Kellogg's puts the raisins *inside* the little bisquits, it tastes different. Boy, you grew up surrounded by maids, country clubs, Republicans. How'd you learn to be such a niggling little pennypincher?

JENNY. It's called good money management. And the way you waste it, you should be down on your knees thanking Mother for teaching me. *(She Exits.)*

BUDDY. Do me one favor, when it comes time for my funeral, don't take bids. Just shove me in the trash masher. *(to the audience:)* She's so damn practical, and organized! It's like being married to a *Volvo!* *(JENNY Enters in a Laura Ashley dress.)* I hate that dress. Where do you buy those things, off a covered wagon?

JENNY. *(She laughs, then defensively.)* This happens to be a Laura Ashley.

BUDDY. Right, official uniform for "Virgins International." It should come with a little warning label. *(pretending to read a label)* "Caution, sex may induce nausea."

JENNY. *(She smiles, making the bed.)* I always enjoy your little fashion commentary, but I've got to drop Sally at her friend's and I'm due at Dr. Pines at ten.

BUDDY. For what? What's the matter?

JENNY. Dr. Pines, the psychologist. He's testing Andy today. Remember Andy? He's your four-year-old?

BUDDY. I *knew* that. I mean about Andy's tests. I just forgot the doctor's name.

JENNY. Buddy, I'm tired of doing this alone.

BUDDY. You're not doing it alone, Jen. If you really want me to skip work today, I will.

JENNY. Nobody wanted them. *(JENNY points to his cereal.)* Eat your breakfast. I don't know why you can't take the time to come downstairs and eat with Sally and Andy. It's the only time they get to see you.

BUDDY. I said good morning in the bathroom. *(She stares at him accusingly.)* You're right, I'll do it tomorrow. Please stand straight. Bad posture is not very sexy.

JENNY. *(picking up his socks)* Neither are your socks on the floor. Are these clean or dirty?

BUDDY. I don't know, smell 'em.

JENNY. *(She starts to sniff, stops.)* I am not your sock smeller. *(She tosses the socks at him.)*

BUDDY. This peach is bruised.

JENNY. It's not that bruised.

BUDDY. It's one big bruise. You've been shopping in the back of the market again, in "the old age home for fruit."

JENNY. Peaches are a dollar nine a pound. I got a giant bag for seventy-five cents.

BUDDY. Good deal and no teeth marks. *(He looks at cereal bowl.)* You bought me the wrong cereal.

JENNY. I did not. It's Spoon Size Shredded Wheat.

BUDDY. I didn't ask for "Spoon Size Shredded Wheat." That's Nabisco. I asked for "Raisin Squares," by Kellogg's. *(He pulls on chino pants.)*

JENNY. *(She pours raisins from a box into his bowl.)* Raisins. I'm not spending an extra ninety eight cents a box, for ten cents worth of raisins. Anyway, the Spoon Size Shredded Wheat was on special at $1.98 *and* double coupon.

love song. BUDDY dances with confidence all around the room.) It's dancing with *women* I'm not very good at. Mmm, that music. After you've heard a love song by Gershwin or Berlin, you want to *kill* Barry Manilow. My mother's the one who got me hooked on those great love songs. She sang them all to me, when I was too young to resist. *(He sings, as if to a baby, a Thirties love song.)*

(JENNY Enters with bed linens and a tray with cereal in a bowl and a very bruised peach. She hands BUDDY a pen and paper.)

JENNY. Here, I need your signature on this.

BUDDY. Honey, you are crippling me creatively. *(He signs the paper and hands it back.)* There you go.

JENNY. Aren't you going to read it?

BUDDY. You read it, why do I have to read it?

JENNY. You're doing a very worthwhile thing. You just became an organ donor.

BUDDY. *(He reacts, leaps to her and reads the paper.)* Are you crazy? You just gave away my heart and my liver!

JENNY. They only remove things after you don't need them.

BUDDY. Who knows *what* I'll need when I get where I'm going?

JENNY. You don't believe in life after death.

BUDDY. Sure, *now,* but I plan to get very religious right before I die. Just don't touch anything else. Thanks for not giving away my nuts.

JENNY. You promised to put a faucet that works in our bathroom.

BUDDY. Faucet, right. Next?

JENNY. You ran the dishwasher again, with only half a load.

BUDDY. I went a little crazy. I owe you three cents worth of "Cascade."

JENNY. Don't forget to vote today.

BUDDY. *(unenthused)* Oh, we're voting again? Alright.

JENNY. *(She gives him a small pamphlet.)* I marked a sample ballot for you. I want you to get Daddy's old tux altered to fit you, *today.*

BUDDY. Christ, do I have to wear a tux to that party?

JENNY. No, go as you are. It's only my mother and Daddy's thirty-fifth anniversary. They hired Russ David's Dance Band.

BUDDY. Oh shit, that probably means dancing.

JENNY. Naturally. You told me yourself, your idol George Gershwin was a wonderful dancer.

BUDDY. Forget it. You knew I couldn't dance when you married me. I can only turn to the left. What are you doing? *(She is picking up the mess on the floor.)*

JENNY. Fighting disease.

BUDDY. Jenny, *don't.* I've got everything where I want it. When you straighten, I can't find a thing.

JENNY. I want this epidemic out of here! *(JENNY Exits.)*

BUDDY. Actually, I dance great. *(We hear a lively Thirties*

BUDDY. I'm getting dressed as fast as I can. *Pan* over to George Gershwin as he sits down at the piano, to play "Rhapsody in Blue."

JENNY. *(O.S.)* It's nine twenty three.

BUDDY. Thank you. *(to the audience:)* George Gershwin, what a guy. He grew up on the streets of New York. Played baseball, got in fights. But when it came to his music, he was a genius. His parents were Russian immigrants, like my mom. Are you ready for this? George was only twenty six when he wrote "Rhasody in Blue." *(unhappily)* I'm thirty five.

(JENNY APPLE [33] enters, wearing very little makeup, in a worn out, unsexy summer robe. She's loaded with men's underwear and socks, which she puts in a dresser drawer. NOTE: JENNY is organized and efficient, but she is not a drudge. She has a great laugh and is alternately amused at BUDDY'S humor and vexed at his unruly life style.)

JENNY. *Buddy.* We agreed, you were going to type on the dining room table.

BUDDY. I'm trying to seize the moment. *(He pinches her behind.)*

JENNY. I'm trying to strip the bed.

BUDDY. So go ahead, strip it. *(He lifts typewriter, she strips bed.)*

JENNY. And I have a lot of things to go over with you.

BUDDY. Oh oh, it's "list time" again.

ALMOST PERFECT

ACT I

As the audience settles down, we hear a love song from the Thirties. LIGHTS dim to black, as the song continues.

AT RISE: We hear a TYPEWRITER. LIGHTS up to reveal BUDDY APPLE (35) in dress shirt and undershorts, typing on a double bed in Jenny's bedroom. We also see end tables and a small dresser and/or dressing table. Papers and clothes are strewn on the floor. He pulls the paper out and reads it.

BUDDY. "1933." A screenplay. Cut to: the skyline of Manhattan in the Thirties. Cut to: The Chrysler Building. Cut to the lights of Broadway. Cut to: ... Nah, that's too much "cutting to." *(A brilliant idea! He smiles.) Dissolve* to a party at George Gershwin's penthouse apartment, *(He pencils in the new word.)* where guests, Ernest Hemingway, Irving Berlin and Dorothy Parker are sharing some literate conversation.

JENNY. *(O.S.)* Buddy, don't you have to leave for work?

I promised his Holiness two free acres and he promised me a church and a school. And you know Italian Catholics. Before you can blink, a dozen kids. *(indicating many little heads)* Maria Christina, Maria Teresa, Maria Maria. And soon they'll be running out of bedrooms, which *we* will be glad to supply. And the Madonna keeps smiling, and *we* keep smiling.

BUDDY. Aren't you forgetting something?
DAD. What?
BUDDY. We're *Jewish.*
DAD. So was the Madonna.

(MIKE Enters unrolling a blueprint.)

BUDDY. Mike, what do *you* think of "Madonna Lakes Estates?"
DAD. Mike's opinion doesn't matter anymore.
BUDDY. What do you mean?
DAD. You didn't tell your brother?
MIKE. I was about to. I told Dad and Mom this morning. I'm leaving to start my own project.
BUDDY. You're bailing out? Jesus Christ! Why?
MIKE. I just want to try things on my own. But I'll stick around as long as I'm needed. Dad, I'm not gonna leave you high and dry.
DAD. You leave *me* high and dry? That'll be the day. I wasn't exactly falling on my ass before I took you in. Bud, we'll talk later about your taking over Mike's duties.
BUDDY. *(unenthused)* Yeah, okay.
DAD. We'll also talk about your new salary.
BUDDY. New Salary?

DAD. You'll be getting more. You'll deserve it. Buddy, be thinking about the ad champaign for Madonna Lakes Estates. Whatever you want, it's your baby. Listen, what do you say, we try a little radio this time?

BUDDY. Radio? I don't know, I've checked it out and...

DAD. *(He interrupts, squeezing BUDDY'S cheek.)* Good, don't forget what you wanted to say. Y'know, I heard them advertising Brentwood Oaks on Mom's psychologist, "Dr. Susan." And those shmucks are selling houses.

BUDDY. Okay, I'll check it out.

DAD. I already did. I mean they contacted me. I told them advertising is your baby. Someone's coming out to see you. *(He pulls a paper from BUDDY'S open briefcase.)* Is this the sales report I asked you for?

BUDDY. No, Dad.

DAD. *(He reads, confused.)* Cut to the skyline of Manhattan in the thirties. What the hell is this?

BUDDY. Nothing, it's a screenplay I'm working on.

DAD. A screenplay? Buddy, for Christ sake! You're in the *building* business.

BUDDY. You know I only write in my spare time.

DAD. Spare time? I wish I had some of that. With him leaving, I have to be able to count on you to be a mensch.

BUDDY. Don't worry, I'm not gonna let you down.

DAD. I'll hold you to that. By the way, "Mr. Words," I loved your flowery descriptions in the brochure. *(to MIKE:)* Who but your brother could make a square hole in a roof sound like a desirable feature? He called it an "atrium." *(MIKE playfully gives BUDDY the finger, behind DAD's back. Then, as DAD turns back, MIKE scratches his cheek to cover up.)* Smart. It's even Italian. I'll be at the downtown office if you need me. Remember, Buddy, think Italian. Ciao. *(DAD Exits.)*

BUDDY. Mike how can you do this to me? You know *I* was thinking about getting outta here, so I can write. You can't just take off and leave me alone with him.

MIKE. Bud, I had to get out of here while I still know how to make a decision. What's the difference what I'm doing? You're thirty-five years old. Do what you want.

BUDDY. You make it sound so simple. How can I leave him now? He calls us his good right arm and his good left arm.

MIKE. Easy, you walk up to him and say, "Listen, *Stumps.*"

BUDDY. Yeah, fine, go ahead, joke. I'm stuck here. I have no control over my life. You're doing it to me again, Mike. First you leave Laura, now this.

MIKE. What's the difference if I left Laura?

BUDDY. Because, I'd like a few options around here, myself. If you want to know, I'm not that happy at home.

MIKE. You're shitting me. You and Jenny are having problems?

BUDDY. No. But that doesn't mean I'm happy.

MIKE. Is that all? Buddy, there's a difference between griping and leaving. My marriage was over. For eight years, I kept giving Laura more rope and she kept taking it. She wants to go into the fucking *rope* business. You and Jenny'll be fine.

BUDDY. I don't want to be fine, I want to be in love.

MIKE. Didn't we have this conversation when you were thirteen? Bud, this is not a "sock hop," it's life. You'll be okay. Just don't fight it so much.

BUDDY. That's what you used to say when you sat on my head.

MIKE. I'm gonna miss that sense of humor of yours. But I'll be back from time to time, when I visit Lot Eighty Three.

BUDDY. Eighty Three? The one with the tits?

MIKE. Yeah, she comes with the standard equipment.

BUDDY. You fell on that? You bastard. she was *my* customer.

MIKE. So what was stopping you?

BUDDY. I thought about it, but I couldn't go for her. She's so short, and she's got these "Steinway legs." God, I feel sorry for dumpy women, even when they've got big tits. There's no way to hide bad legs. They try pants...

MIKE. *Hey!* Don't ruin it for *me!* I like 'em built healthy and close to the ground. Buddy, as a parting gift, I'm gonna teach you a few things about women. You don't have to fall in love with 'em to bang 'em. And they love builders. Any woman who walks through that door needs me. With these strong hands, I build her shelter. Think of the symbolism. The operative word here is *erection. (He projects the measuring tape on his belt to indicate "erection.")* You've got a sexual role to play, and look how you're dressed.

BUDDY. I'm head of sales.

MIKE. You head's in your ass. You're a *builder.* Dress

like one. Boots, jeans, tan, they eat it up.
  BUDDY. Dad asked me to wear a coat and tie.
  MIKE. Of course he did. Dad doesn't want you to get laid. You want to know why I got Lot Eighty Three and you're playing with yourself?
  BUDDY. Alright, why?
  MIKE. A couple of months ago I walk in the office and there she is. I'd been backfilling with the dozer that day, so I had a hint of diesel about me. She's going through sheer torture trying to decide on her kitchen group colors. Sandalwood ... *or* ... Avocado? Y'see, women tend to be slightly insecure. Probably from waiting in line at public toilets. So, I took charge, and said, "Hi, I'm the builder. Why don't I help you decide?" and I move in close, so my elbow's touching her tit. *(MIKE'S arm touches BUDDY'S chest.)* Elbow to brain: *Soft*.
  BUDDY. Jesus, what did she do?
  MIKE. Nothing. She just had to step back an inch if she wasn't interested. She didn't budge. Her husband travels.
  BUDDY. I wouldn't have the nerve to touch some strange tit. Anyway, I'm not looking to screw around. That gets everything very complicated. Look what happened to you and Laura.
  MIKE. I take great offense at that. My screwing around had nothing to do with our problems. It was the twelve years of unbroken screaming. I can still hear it in sea shells.
  BUDDY. Jenny and I never scream. We never even *fight*. We just peck at each other.
  MIKE. How is she in bed?

BUDDY. You shithead.

MIKE. That bad, huh?

BUDDY. No, she's fine, once I get her there. But it's always *me* asking *her*. I'm constantly saying to myself, "Okay, this time *she's* gonna ask. If it takes weeks ... months ... years. I'm saying *nothing* till she asks. I've waited as long as *five* days.

MIKE. Five days? Snails don't wait that long! *(He pats BUDDY on the back.)* Well, at least you know Jenny doesn't screw around.

BUDDY. Yeah, no problem there. She doesn't know how to flirt. She doesn't wear makeup. She dresses like Emily Dickenson. What guy is gonna come on to Jenny, unless he needs voting information?

("BOOTS" CLARK [30], beautiful, blonde, Enters, carrying a briefcase. She is dressed appropriate for business but sexy enough to be appreciated by men.)

BOOTS. Hello, is this the sales office?

MIKE. It sure is. Hi, I'm the builder.

BOOTS. Mr. Apple?

MIKE. That's right. And you are?

BOOTS. Boots Clark, KPRZ.

BUDDY. Oh, Ms. Clark, I'm...

MIKE. *Bud,* I got it. *(to BOOTS:)* Now, you're the type of customer that makes building a pleasure. Obviously an intelligent, capable, career gal moving up fast. *(He walks her to a floor plan.)* Why don't you step right over here? I'll explain what Apple Construction is all about. This is the ideal first house for you. Two spacious bedrooms, a fully

tiled bath. Very sexy kitchen in either Sandalwood or Avocado. *(His elbow touches BOOTS' breast. She steps back.)*
BOOTS. Lovely.
BUDDY. *Jesus!*
BOOTS. But I'm not interested ... in a house. In fact, I don't think you're the person I want to talk to.
MIKE. I'm the builder.
BOOTS. The foreman told me to look for Buddy Apple, a man in a sportcoat and tie.
BUDDY. *(His hand shoots up happily.)* Yo! I'm Buddy Apple. See, sportcoat, tie?
BOOTS. *(Smiles, warmly, shakes BUDDY'S hand.)* Hi, I'm Boots Clark, from KPRZ.
BUDDY. Hi.
BOOTS. Hi, I'd love to talk to you about the impact of radio advertising.

(JENNY picks up a phone in limbo)

JENNY. *(into the phone:)* Hello?

JENNY. *(into the phone:)* Hi, Mother.

BOOTS. I apologize for being so late.
BUDDY. I've got all the time in the world.
MIKE. Bud, I've got some important overall supervising to do, so I'll just...
BUDDY. Good, Mike. And report back to me later. *(MIKE reacts at "being had," then Exits.)*

JENNY. *(into the phone:)* No, Buddy's not home yet.

BOOTS. Your dad said advertising is your baby.

BUDDY. That's right. *(BUDDY leads BOOTS to the office desk. They sit. BOOTS opens her briefcase.)*

JENNY. *(into the phone:)* Of course, Buddy voted today, Mother. Thanks for keeping the kids tonight. Andy's tests? Nothing new. Difficult behavior patterns, short attention span. The same stuff they always tell me. No, Buddy couldn't go. He had some really important things at the office.

(LIGHTS dim out on JENNY. She Exits.)

BOOTS. *(laughing)* That's very funny.

BUDDY. You like that?

BOOTS. Yes. You're the funniest builder I've talked to today. Anyway, I'd say your best buy would be drive-time spots during Dr. Susan's late afternoon show. How does that sound, Mr. Apple?

BUDDY. Perfect, except my father is "Mr. Apple." I'm Bud. *(She laughs.)* You find that funny, too? *(to the audience:)* Hey, I'm doing okay here.

BOOTS. *(still enjoying it)* Don't mind me, I'm a nut. "Bud" is kind of a joke name I use for my boyfriend, Pete, when he works too hard. Y'see, he's an executive at Anheuser Busch. *Bud.*

BUDDY. Oh? Well, we've got to call me something. How about Buddy, or Heineken or Schlitz? *(She laughs, showing beautiful teeth.)* My compliments to your orthodontist.

BOOTS. I didn't have one. *(She points heavenward.)* Other than *him.*

BUDDY. My compliments to *Him. (He points heavenward.)* He did an excellent job. On *everything.*

BOOTS. Thank you.

(MIKE Enters.)

MIKE. Buddy, I'm leaving. It's six, aren't you going to be late for dinner with your *wife?*

BUDDY. *(He looks at the audience, caught.)* Oh, that's right.

BOOTS. Is it six already? Pete'll kill me. Now that I've seen your operation, I'll lay out a campaign, then we'll talk. No obligation.

BUDDY. Oh, let me be a little obligated.

MIKE. It's dark out there, Boots. C'mon, I'll walk you to your car.

BOOTS. Thanks. Goodbye, Bud.

MIKE. Goodbye, Bud. Boots, did you ever take a ride on a dozer? *(MIKE and BOOTS Exit.)*

BUDDY. *(to the audience:)* He couldn't be my brother. A second cousin wouldn't do that.

(We hear our interlude MUSIC.)

BUDDY. Boots Clark. Unbelievable. She reminds me so much of Carole Lombard. *The* movie beauty of the thirties. Carole Lombard. *She's* the reason I dream in black and white.

(The MUSIC ends. BUDDY walks through limbo to JENNY'S bedroom.)

JENNY. Buddy, is that you?
BUDDY. Yeah, sorry I'm late.
JENNY. *(O.S.)* You could've called.
BUDDY. That would've made me later. Are the kids at your mother's?

(JENNY Enters, changing to a blouse and full skirt.)

JENNY. Yes. I called your Mom and told her we'd be very late.
BUDDY. How'd it go with Andy?
JENNY. Okay. There's nothing new. I'll tell you in the car. I called you at the office and got the answering machine. I guess you'd already left to vote?
BUDDY. Actually, no. I completely ran out of time.
JENNY. I knew it, Buddy! You're disgraceful. Mother asked if you'd voted. I lied to her.
BUDDY. And you lied to my father this morning. That's a bad habit.
JENNY. You take it so lightly. Voting happens to be more than a right and a privilege, it's a duty. Hitler got into power because people like you didn't vote.
BUDDY. I apologize for letting Hitler in. It won't happen again. Come here. *(He kisses her.)*
JENNY. Couldn't you have left the office a half hour earlier?
BUDDY. When Mike tells me he's leaving the firm, I think it's worth a few minutes discussion.

JENNY. Mike's leaving?

BUDDY. Yes. He's starting his own project. And then I had a very important advertising meeting.

JENNY. Was it more important than voting?

BUDDY. *(to the audience:)* Is she kidding? It was more important than *citizenship*.

JENNY. How the hell could you not vote?

BUDDY. Hitler wasn't running this time. It was a nothing election. *(He begins removing his sportcoat and shirt and gets into a sportshirt.)*

JENNY. That's not true. My friend Nancy Krakower winning a seat on the Board of Education is very important.

BUDDY. Nancy Krakower? Aren't there enough ugly women on that board already?

JENNY. *(Shakes her head, fighting a smile.)* That's not funny.

BUDDY. I know. Especially for her husband. Tell you what, we'll stop on the way to Mom and Dad's and I'll vote, okay?

JENNY. *(softening)* Okay. I finished my little speech for the anniversary party. Want to hear it?

BUDDY. Yeah, go ahead. *(He Exits, then comes back wiping his face with a wash cloth, holding a brush for his hair.)*

JENNY. *(She reads "sincerely," from a paper.)* Mother and Daddy: On this happy occasion of your thirty-fifth anniversary, I want to thank you both for setting wonderful examples for me. Your intense involvement in the St. Louis community has always given me inspiration and demonstrated that being a viable community leader is not only gratifying and fulfilling... *(BUDDY has been react-*

ing to the "good citizen" tedium of her speech. He interrupts with a snore.)

BUDDY. Wait a minute. Have you been introduced to these people? They're your parents. Write something cute. Be adorable.

JENNY. You're right. You'll have to help me. Are you ready? I'm starved. Your mom told me she baked lemon pound cake.

BUDDY. Fine, but let's be aware of the possibility of something nice happening later. If it so pleases you? *(He lays down in a comic pose, waving at her with his fingers.)*

JENNY. Something nice? That's a possibility.

BUDDY. *(bluntly, as he moves to her)* Good. We're talking *definite penetration* here, so please, D.O.E. Don't overeat.

JENNY. I'm not going to overeat and I don't want you staring at me. I didn't have time for lunch and I'm very hungry.

BUDDY. Fine, I only mention it, because I know how you love my mother's cooking. *(to the audience:)* And I don't want a beached whale on my hands.

JENNY. *(an anticipatory smile)* She's making her stuffed peppers.

BUDDY. Just remember how uncomfortable you get.

JENNY. *(Smiles, as she brushes her hair.)* Yeah.

BUDDY. And remember one other thing. Priorities.

JENNY. You mean, sex.

BUDDY. I mean, breathing. Last time, you asked to have dessert served in an oxygen tent. And what fun when we got home. *(He lays down and comically dem-*

onstrates.) You laying there, gasping for air, begging me to take your shoes off. Then, the final thrill, you fell asleep on me.

JENNY. I won't fall asleep. And if I do, we'll make it up in the morning.

BUDDY. *(He rises, making the point of his life.)* You *never* make 'em up! Once they're *gone,* they're *gone!* And it's been five days.

JENNY. It's so romantic to have love making on a schedule.

BUDDY. Some schedule. We were going to get together Monday night, until your "Smoking Kills" meeting came up. Then Tuesday was Business Economics, Wednesday, Basic Computer Skills...

JENNY. Alright, I had a busy week. I'm trying to get a degree one of these days. We do have the whole weekend.

BUDDY. No we don't. You're getting your period tomorrow.

JENNY. *(amazed)* You know that?! *How?* You have a *headache?*

BUDDY. I happen to have you programmed into my calendar alarm watch. You "dinged" this morning.

JENNY. Here we go again. You do this every month. You actually hold my period against me.

BUDDY. I do not. I'm just trying to face it with you.

JENNY. I want to face it *alone!*

BUDDY. *(tenderly)* Jenny, I know this testing thing with Andy must have been crappy. If you're feeling bummed out, we can forget tonight.

JENNY. No, it was okay and I want to make love.

BUDDY. Wonderful.

JENNY. All this planning is what bums me out.

BUDDY. You're right, no planning. Oh, by the way, good news. We'll have more money, when I take over Mike's job.

JENNY. Great.

BUDDY. Y'know, we could bring the lemon pound cake back here and have it after we make ... sorry.

JENNY. We'll just let things happen. Ready?

BUDDY. You're very pretty, you know that? Nice slim hips, somewhere under that Mother Goose skirt. Outstanding nose job. Great legs, too. Let me check something. *(He sits her on the bed, then grabs her ankle.)*

JENNY. What are you doing?

BUDDY. This is how Harold Minsky of Minsky's Burlesque picked perfect legs. Thin ankles are very important. If he could touch his thumb and middle finger together, the legs were perfect. *(He can't quite touch.)* See that? Almost perfect. *(He smiles and sings a love song from the Thirties. For example:)*

DON'T BLAME ME FOR FALLING IN LOVE WITH YOU.

I'M UNDER YOUR SPELL, BUT HOW CAN I HELP IT. DON'T BLAME ME

(He puts his arm around her. They Exit.)

(LIGHTS up on MOM and DAD'S dining room. MOM APPLE [60], in a dress and apron, Enters, setting the table, which can be brought on by actors.)

MOM. *(singing a continuation of BUDDY's love song)*
CAN'T YOU SEE, WHEN YOU DO THE THINGS YOU DO.

IF I CAN'T CONCEAL THE THRILL THAT I'M FEELING...

(JENNY, carrying a bag from Saks, and BUDDY Enter.)

JENNY. Hi Mom, sorry we're late. *(She points meaningfully to BUDDY.)*
BUDDY. Hi, Mom. *(He hugs MOM.)*
MOM. Hi, Sweetheart.

(DAD Enters, rolled up sleeves, chewing a cigar.)

DAD. Hi, kids.
JENNY. Dad! What is that in your mouth?
DAD. I'm not smoking, I'm biting.
JENNY. Good, I brought you something. *(She hands him a news clipping.)*
DAD. *(Smiles, to MOM.)* Jenny brought me something. *(He glances at the clipping, forces a smile.)* An article on mouth cancer. How thoughtful.
JENNY. This house smells wonderful.
MOM. Wait till you taste it. I hope you're hungry.
BUDDY. Was tonight for dinner? We already ate. *(MOM reacts, then laughs.)*
MOM. Such a wonderful jokester. He likes to make his mother laugh. *(taking JENNY'S paper bag, MOM removes a conservative one-piece woman's swim suit)* Good, you brought the swim suit.
BUDDY. So that's what you were hiding in the bag?
JENNY. I knew you'd hate it.
MOM. It's beautiful. I'd like to have it myself.

BUDDY. It's too old for you, Mom.

JENNY. *(holding the suit up to her chest)* Could you take it in through the neck? It just hangs there.

MOM. I'll try. I've never taken in a bathing suit.

DAD. You've never had to.

MOM. Dear, we're given what God gives us.

BUDDY. No wonder you believe in God.

DAD. *(joking, he nuzzles her)* This is what I've been up against all these years. My first wife. Got her right off the boat. I always have something to fall back on. *(DAD gives MOM an unseen goose.)*

MOM. Stop it. Go away.

DAD. I love to make her blush. *(to JENNY:)* Jenny, how about some white wine? It's in the kitchen.

JENNY. Good, I want to peek in the oven. *(JENNY and DAD Exit.)*

BUDDY. *(for JENNY'S benefit)* Don't fall in, Gretel.

MOM. *(to BUDDY:)* Why do you make her so nervous about what she wears?

BUDDY. I just want her to look her best.

MOM. Men, always with the looks.

BUDDY. Lucky for you. If you weren't so gorgeous, you'd still be sewing for the gentiles in Kiev. You told me yourself, the border guards let your family out of Russia because they thought you were cute.

MOM. *(enjoying this "truth")* That's true, because men are fools. I don't know what they all see in me.

BUDDY. Mom, men have this weakness. They love beautiful women. I'm talking about intelligent men, sensitive men. Arthur Miller married Marilyn Monroe, didn't he? And Eleanor Roosevelt was *very* available.

MOM. Your Jenny just happens to be a lovely girl.
BUDDY. I agree.
MOM. Then tell her that. I like to give people flowers while they can still smell them. And give her a pinch once in a while, the way Dad always bothers me.

(MIKE Enters.)

MIKE. Hi, Mom.
MOM. Michael, darling. *(She kisses MIKE.)*
MIKE. Hi, Bud.
BUDDY. Mike. *(MIKE purses his lips at BUDDY.)* No thanks.
MOM. *(She calls O.S.)* Dear, Michael's here. Let's all sit down.
MIKE. How you feeling, Mom?
MOM. I'll feel fine, if you and Dad get along tonight.
MIKE. That's up to him and you know it.
MOM. Just keep food in your mouth, not answers. *(MOM Exits.)*
MIKE. If he starts, I'm leaving. I can't take any more of his crap.
BUDDY. Sure you can. Come on, take some crap for Mom. *(He playfully punches MIKE'S arm.)*
MIKE. That didn't hurt. *(as he walks away, he hits BUDDY'S arm.)*

(DAD and JENNY Enter with wine. JENNY is chewing bread.)

DAD. Jenny, I should tell someone with a down payment in his hand that he can't smoke in my sales office?

JENNY. You don't have to tell them. Just put up a small "No Smoking" sign. Mmm, Mom this onion garlic bread is delicious.

BUDDY. *(He reacts. Then, to JENNY.)* Dinner didn't even start. You're eating already? *(He chuckles hollowly.)*

MIKE. Hi, Dad.

DAD. Michael, you're here. Now maybe we can start.

JENNY. Hiya, Mike. *(JENNY hugs MIKE. DAD starts pouring ice tea for JENNY, then BUDDY.)*

DAD. Y'see, Jenny, things are going to be tough enough on this project. Buddy and I are faced with developing fifty acres, by *ourselves*. Just the two of us, *alone*.

(Instead of pouring MIKE some tea, DAD slams the pitcher down firmly, next to him. MOM Enters with a platter of potato pancakes. They sit for dinner.)

MOM. Potato pancakes?

BUDDY. Just one for me, Mom.

MOM. One? Since when?

BUDDY. It's summertime, Jenny and I are eating light, so we won't feel stuffed.

JENNY. *Two* for me, Mom. Mike, I hear you're starting your own project. Good luck.

MIKE. Thanks, Jenny. *(MOM Exits to the kitchen.)*

BUDDY. And lucky for us, he bought acreage on the

North Side, so we won't be competing.

DAD. Of course we'll be competing. If not on this project, the next. That's fine, I'm not afraid of competition.

JENNY. Sour cream? *(MIKE passes JENNY the sour cream. She piles it on her plate as BUDDY reacts.* NOTE: *During this entire scene, JENNY eats with delight and total gusto.)*

DAD. So, when are you leaving officially, Michael? I don't want to be surprised again..

MIKE. I didn't surprise you. I told you, "I'd like to leave."

DAD. It's *when* you told me. *After* the three of us agreed to take on this new development.

(MOM Enters with a bowl of noodles.)

JENNY. Mmm, noodles! *(She takes a large helping as BUDDY reacts.)*

MIKE. Dad face it. Some people weren't meant to work together.

DAD. Dear, our son just made a big discovery. I'm impossible to work with.

MIKE. I didn't say that.

MOM. I leave the room for ten seconds!

DAD. *(to MIKE:)* It's just a shame you couldn't have come to me, like a mensch, *before* I bought the fifty acres and said, "Goodbye, Dad, I've picked your brain for fourteen years, now I'm leaving."

MOM. *(She feels her side, pained.)* Mmmph!

DAD. What's the matter? Your gallstone operation again?

MOM. You know it hurts me when you fight. Michael is our son.

DAD. No, we got him on sale at K-Mart. Of course he's our son.

JENNY. Mom, I'll serve. Why don't you sit down?

MOM. If I sit down, there goes my diet. *(MOM Exits.)*

DAD. If he *weren't* our son, I'd be suing him for sticking me with fifty acres of corn and alfalfa.

MIKE. *(to DAD:)* Why are you so angry? You were in business with Grandpa and you left to go on your own.

JENNY. *(to BUDDY:)* The bread please?

DAD. That's right, I left, with Pa's blessing. I didn't run away. You've got a history of running away from things.

MIKE. Can we skip the history lessons?

DAD. *(touching his stomach)* It can only stay in here so long. When I caught you smoking at eleven and I grounded you, you ran to Cincinnati, hitchhiking.

BUDDY. *(He hands JENNY a small heel of bread.)* Sweetie, starches tend to swell, *later*.

JENNY. *(She takes a larger piece.)* I'll worry about that, *later*.

(MOM Enters with a baking dish of stuffed peppers, which she hands to JENNY, then Exits.)

JENNY. Ooh, the *peppers*.
BUDDY. And they're *stuffed*.
DAD. Then there were more people you couldn't get

along with. The entire Marine Corps. So you went AWOL.
MIKE. For *one* day!
DAD. Because they *caught* you. Suddenly your marriage isn't working, off you run. Now, you've got a problem with me, so once again you're putting on your track shoes!
MIKE. If you say so.
DAD. I *say so!*
MOM. *(O.S.)* I'm not coming in, until I hear it quiet.

(After a beat, MOM Enters with a bowl. She moves to MIKE as he pushes his plate away.)

MOM. Michael, you're not eating?
MIKE. I'm not hungry, Mom.
MOM. Buddy's not eating, Mike's not eating. Thank God for Jenny. *(MOM grabs a bowl and Exits.)*
JENNY. *(spearing MIKE'S potato pancake)* Mike, I can't let this pancake go to waste.
BUDDY. Honey, *D.O.E.*
JENNY. Honey, *P.T.B.*
BUDDY. What?
JENNY. Pass the butter.
BUDDY. No! Are you aware that the whale is an endangered species?
JENNY. Really? That will leave a lot of *whalers* with their harpoons in their *hands*, won't it?

(The LIGHTS go dark on everyone but BUDDY. He rises and walks into limbo.)

BUDDY. *(to the audience)* What a night. Maybe it was the heat. July in St. Louis. The Gershwins never thought to write a song about that. Humidity? You need scuba equipment to breathe. Temperature? Ninety five degrees, at *night*. And in the car with Jenny on the way home, *ice* formed on the windshield.

(LIGHTS up on JENNY and BUDDY'S bedroom. JENNY is lying, totally stuffed, on the bed. Her eyes have lost their focus. BUDDY moves to the bed.)

BUDDY. *(kicking off his shoes, miffed)* I hope you enjoyed dinner.

JENNY. Immensely.

BUDDY. Hope you aren't as miserable as you look.

JENNY. Thanks for your concern. Don't worry, we'll do it.

BUDDY. Wow, there's an attitude that's dizzy with excitement.

JENNY. Maybe that's because I'm feeling a bit more like a piece of meat than usual.

BUDDY. Lucky I had nothing to do with that.

JENNY. You know what *would* make me dizzy with excitement? A guy who didn't treat me like a maid. *(She rises, picks up his socks.)* You want passion? Show me someone who's responsible enough to vote without being told. A guy who might take off work for a day, when his son really needs him. *(She picks up his shoes and slams them down on a chair.)*

BUDDY. Oh boy. This guy you're describing wouldn't need genitals, would he? Because mine just turned to *con-*

crete. I'll try to bump into anything. *(He starts Exiting, his walk exaggerated, as though he has a block of concrete between his legs.)*

JENNY. Where are you going?

BUDDY. Downstairs, to get something to eat. *I* didn't *stuff* myself. Y'know, I never thought I'd say this, but I'm out of the mood. Just plain burned out from trying to build a fire under you.

JENNY. You wouldn't need to build a fire if I felt you were trying to be a partner around here.

BUDDY. See, everything's conditional with you. If I'm a good boy, suddenly a miracle will happen and you'll become loving and passionate and maybe initiate things around here once in awhile.

JENNY. That's possible.

BUDDY. Anything's possible. But I don't think I should have to work so hard to have a loving wife.

JENNY. I am a loving wife, goddamit!

BUDDY. Goodnight, Jennifer. *(BUDDY Exits, walks to limbo.)*

JENNY. *(calling after him)* I'll be asleep when you get back.

BUDDY. *(O.S.)* So what else is new?

(We hear a romantic song from the Thirties.)

BUDDY. *(as he puts on socks and shoes)* Back in the thirties, they wrote the perfect song for every mood. I wonder if anyone ever wrote one called, "MY WIFE IS A PAIN IN THE ASS?" What happened after that had nothing to do with my argument with Jenny. It just kind of started, at this perfectly innocent, totally valid business lunch. I had to give Boots some bad news. Instead of buying ten thousand dollars worth of radio time for "Madonna Lakes Estates," as *she* had suggested, I was going to buy eight hundred dollars worth, as *Dad* had suggested. And she just smiled at me and said, "No problem."

(A LIGHT comes up on BOOTS, in a restaurant. BUDDY joins her.)

BOOTS. *(in concert with BUDDY)* No problem.
BUDDY. Are you sure? I hate to take bread out of such a lovely mouth.
BOOTS. How thoughtful. But it's only money. Besides, I have a trust fund, *plus* "Victor the Vulture."
BUDDY. Victor the Vulture? Who's that, your lawyer?
BOOTS. No, that's the name of a children's book that I wrote and illustrated.
BUDDY. What a talent! How clever, doing a kid's book about a disgusting animal. Why don't you make your next hero, "Leonard the Leech?" A very depressed little leech who thinks the whole world sucks?
BOOTS. *(She laughs.)* What a wonderful idea. May I steal it?
BUDDY. It's yours. Y'know, I'm a writer too.
BOOTS. You are?
BUDDY. Yeah, I'm writing a screenplay about New York in the Thirties and people like George Gershwin and Dorothy Parker.

BOOTS. How interesting. Tell me about it.
BUDDY. *(to the audience:)* And we just talked and laughed all afternoon... about writing and art and music. And the next day we had lunch again, and the next day again. We feel the same way about so many things. You're not gonna believe this, but she loves Gershwin almost as much as I do.
BOOTS. *(with naive enthisiasm)* I think Jews are *so* creative.
BUDDY. *(enthused, to the audience:)* Isn't that cute? She's not the least bit anti-semitic. *(to BOOTS: checking his watch)* Jesus, it's four o'clock. Is that a problem for you?
BOOTS. I'm with a client, right?
BUDDY. Right.

(LIGHTS dim on restaurant. LIGHTS up on JENNY'S bedroom, as she makes the bed in robe and nightgown [finding a child's toy], as DAD's RADIO commercial comes on.)

DAD'S VOICE. *(accompanied by Italian folk MUSIC)* This is Norman Apple of Apple Construction, inviting you to come out to "Madonna Lakes Estates," the most exciting new real estate development since Venice. Six spacious new model homes. Circle the date, August 18th. Madonna Lakes Estates Grand Opening and Italian Festival. Take a ride in a genuine Italian gondola. Take a taste of the world's largest pizza, that we're baking up on our parking lot. August 18th, see you there. *(He chuckles.)* Gratz-ee-ay.

(The TELEPHONE rings on "Circle the date.")

JENNY. *(into phone)* Hello? — Hi. — Yes, I'm listening. Let's hear the end of it. — *(She waits for the commercial to end.)* Wasn't it good? — Of course Buddy wrote it, Mother. — I'll tell him for you. He's still at the office. — Well, not every night, but it gets very hectic, leading up to a grand opening. — I'm terrific, now that the kids are finally in bed. — Listen, remember when you said you were going to leave me that big diamond pin in your will? Could you leave me full-time help, instead?

(LIGHTS dim on JENNY'S bedroom. LIGHTS up on restaurant. BUDDY wears a tie. BOOTS adds a jacket to denote evening wear.)

BUDDY. You have no idea how much I've looked forward to this. I've been breathing cement dust all day, supervising foundations.

BOOTS. You're in charge of construction too? You're amazing.

BUDDY. I know. Boots. *(He holds her hand.)*

BOOTS. Yes?

BUDDY. Ignore me. I just love saying your name.

BOOTS. It's a silly name. I was a stable brat at the Hunt Club.

BUDDY. I'll bet the Hunt Club's a terrific place to cantor and post, on a chestnut, like this one? *(He pulls up a pant leg and displays a sock with a horse on it.)*

BOOTS. What cute socks. Nice legs... on the horse. Do you ride?

BUDDY. I used to. When I was a kid, you couldn't get me off a good palomino or Arabian.

BOOTS. Really? Where did you ride?
BUDDY. All over the place. I'm lying.
BOOTS. I know.
BUDDY. I was a street urchin.
BOOTS. That was my guess.
BUDDY. I urched all over the place. But I wasn't lying about loving your name. Very sexy, "Boots." It makes me think of Nazi generals in high heels.
BOOTS. *(She laughs.)* You're very funny.
BUDDY. Thanks. I'm usually tongue-tied around such loveliness. I hope you're not one of those beautiful women who find shallow compliments shallow?
BOOTS. Not at all.
BUDDY. *(looking around the room)* This is just terrific, our first real nighttime date.
BOOTS. See anyone you know?
BUDDY. *No,* I'm just looking around for our waiter ... and my father-in-law, who carries a gun. Isn't this exciting?
BOOTS. Terribly. But I think it's time for me to head home.
BUDDY. First, I want to ask you something. How would you like to go to a fantastic art show, "The Soviet People's Collection of French Impressionists?"
BOOTS. That one from Lenigrad? Marvelous, I love the Impressionists.
BUDDY. Good, these are the real biggies? Eddie M*anay,* Vinnie Van *Go.*
BOOTS. Isn't that exhibition at The Chicago Art Institute?
BUDDY. It sure is.

BOOTS. In Chicago?

BUDDY. That's right, "The Paris of the Plains."

BOOTS. Buddy, that's a pretty big step, don't you think?

BUDDY. Maybe ... I don't know ... *come on.* I'm inviting you for a dream weekend at the Home Builders Convention in a city where not one person knows me. Two days and two nights of theatre, great music, memorable food ... plus one quick look at water heaters, so I can write the whole thing off. Whataya say?

BOOTS. KPRZ wouldn't approve of a weekend in Chicago with a client. Let me think about it. You want a playmate, don't you?

BUDDY. Not just any playmate.

BOOTS. You are so smooth.

BUDDY. Teflon. *(to the audience:)* Sandpaper. I'm a nervous wreck. How does a married man have an affair with a beautiful, classy single girl? Especially when his wife handles the checkbook and wants receipts.

BOOTS. What am I doing with you? A married man is the last thing I need. Everyone knows married men are trouble.

BUDDY. Honest, I'm hardly any trouble at all. Besides, I think I'm falling in love with you.

BOOTS. You are? *(They kiss.)* You'd better be. Y'know, you're not even that good looking.

BUDDY. Darn, you noticed.

BOOTS. Maybe I'm tied of good looking men. I'm not making any promises. I'll think about it and let you know.

BUDDY. Good. When, where, how?

BOOTS. Why don't I just call you ... at your house?
BUDDY. I can hardly wait. *(He chuckles nervously.)*
BOOTS. Stop sweating. I'll be in touch. *(BOOTS Exits into the darkness.)*
BUDDY. *(He rises, enthused. To the audience:)* I finally figured out what love really is. It's getting someone who's too *good* for you. And Boots is so playful. "You're not even that good looking." I *love* being *jerked* around like that. *(serious, to himself:)* Okay, settle down. Before you drive home, think. Check for the obvious things, like ... *(He searches for hairs, finds one.)* long blonde hairs. *(Holds it out, drops it.)* Lipstick smudges. *(Pulls out Kleenex, rubs mouth.)* Dispose of the evidence. *(Balls up Kleenex, drops it.)* Jenny would kill me, if she saw me littering like that. *(He picks up Kleenex.)* Now, the perfume smell. *(He pulls half an onion from a zip-lock bag in his jacket.)* Sliced onion in a zip-lock bag. *(He rubs it on his face, grimaces.)* I've got to check every detail because of this genetic flaw I have. Whenever I lie, I sort of smile. Mike told me, never sneak in like a thief. Enter with confidence and energy ... and pray she's asleep.

(BUDDY crosses to JENNY and BUDDY'S bedroom. LIGHTS up on JENNY, reading a book in bed, in robe and nightgown.)

BUDDY. *(forced bravado)* Good, you're awake. I decided to go out and see this horror movie after work. You would've hated it. But it was just what I needed to get the stress out of my system. *(He sighs stressfully.)*
JENNY. What were you doing at "The Fireside?"
BUDDY. The Fireside? I wasn't at the Fireside. What's the Fireside?

JENNY. The manager called. You forgot to get your Mastercard back when you paid your bill.

BUDDY. The *Fireside?* Is that what they call that place? *(He smiles.)*

JENNY. What's so funny?

BUDDY. The horror movie. When it wasn't terrifying, it was hilarious. I saw "Street of Screams" at Cinema Three. I went in at eight, got out at nine forty five and suddenly I was starved. So I went to the Fireside.

JENNY. All the way down in South St. Louis?

BUDDY. What's so strange about that? *(He smiles.)*

JENNY. Why are you grinning? You're lying, aren't you?

BUDDY. Lying? I'm just glad to see you. Hi. *(He kisses her.)*

JENNY. Ooh! You smell like a big onion!

BUDDY. That's why I went all the way down to the Fireside. They have the best onion rings in town. I'd better wash my face. So, how are the kids? *(He Exits to the bathroom.)*

JENNY. What's the difference? The important thing is, you went to your horror movie, for *six dollars.* You couldn't even wait till it came to the Tivoli and pay three for that garbage. *(BUDDY Enters, towelling his face.)*

BUDDY. Jenny, I promise, somehow I'll make that three dollars up to you.

JENNY. What are you doing with those socks?

BUDDY. What socks?

JENNY. The dirty ones you just put back neatly in your drawer? *(She gets out of bed and gets socks.)*

BUDDY. They're not dirty. I hardly walked today. Most

of the time my feet were up on the desk.

JENNY. These aren't the socks you left home in this morning.

BUDDY. I bought some new socks. Big deal.

JENNY. With horses on them?

BUDDY. I love horses.

JENNY. Since when?

BUDDY. Since *Trigger!*

JENNY. Where are your old socks?

BUDDY. I gave 'em to the *Smithsonian.* I threw 'em out. They were old.

JENNY. Where's the receipt?

BUDDY. What do I need a receipt for? I've got the socks. Jesus, can we get off the subject?

JENNY. Sure. Let's talk about your bill at the Fireside, for $35.50.

BUDDY. You asked the guy what my bill was?

JENNY. How do you eat $35.50 worth of onion rings?

BUDDY. It wasn't all onion rings. I had other stuff.

JENNY. What other stuff?

BUDDY. Christ, I have to be up really early tomorrow to work on Gershwin's trip to Paris. *(He Exits, then re-enters. She stands there, arms folded, staring angrily.)* Okay, you want to know exactly what I had?

JENNY. Yes.

BUDDY. I had soup, I had salad, with *roquefort*, fifty cents extra. I had two shrimp cocktails.

JENNY. Two shrimp cocktails?! At what, five ninety five each?

BUDDY. See that's why I didn't want to tell you.

JENNY. And you know, shrimp is pure cholesterol.

BUDDY. Then I had something really expensive. Lobster, fixed a special way. Almondine, I think.

JENNY. Who ever heard of a lobster with *nuts?*

BUDDY. *(He unbuckles his pants, lets them drop.)* I like 'em crunchy. It wasn't on the menu. I put myself entirely in the waiter's hands. *(impatiently angry, taking off his pants.)* And then I had ... *another* shrimp cocktail. Are we up to $35.50 yet?

JENNY. No! But I'm up to *here* with your bullshit!

BUDDY. I don't think I need your permission to go out to dinner!

JENNY. The *hell* you don't. When you work late at that office, seven days a week. Other people have to be considered. Your family has some rights too. I have some rights.

BUDDY. That's the building business. You've got to sell houses before the interest eats you up.

JENNY. So, you've got salesmen for that.

BUDDY. People want to deal with the prinicpals.

JENNY. So do *I!* I want you home, not running around going to movies by yourself, if you expect me to believe that. I'm sick of being the sole nurse, baby sitter and referee for our kids.

BUDDY. That's what mothers do. I believe it's called raising children.

JENNY. They need parenting, not just mothering. That means both of us.

BUDDY. Okay, I'll talk to Dad about early retirement. That's enough, okay? Goodnight. *(He gets into bed, turns off his lamp.)*

JENNY. *(sarcastically)* Fine.

BUDDY. That's *it,* Jennifer!

JENNY. *(She throws her robe on the floor, gets into bed, turns off her lamp.)* Okay! — Of course, you never want to discuss things that don't interest you, like your kids.

BUDDY. *(He turns on his lamp.)* You've got a lot of goddam nerve saying that. I love my kids. Why the hell do you think I spend all that time out there trying to sell houses?

JENNY. I'm talking about when you're through with work, like tonight. Since when do I have to ask you to come home? People who love each other usually want to spend time together.

BUDDY. Okay, that's a good point. Maybe that's the problem.

JENNY. What's that supposed to mean?

BUDDY. I don't know. Forget it.

JENNY. That's a shitty thing to say. Why don't you just grow up. That would solve our problem.

BUDDY. Growing up doesn't have a thing to do with this.

JENNY. It sure as hell does.

BUDDY. This has to do with the way we feel about each other. The way *I* feel. God, this is tough.

JENNY. *(She afraid to venture further.)* Then let's discuss it tomorrow. We're both tired and angry.

BUDDY. I'm not angry. I wish that were the problem. I don't know.

JENNY. Are you saying ... you don't love me?

BUDDY. I'm not say that. I don't know what I'm saying. — Maybe I am.

JENNY. I can't believe you mean that. Are you trying to hurt me? Because you're doing it. Is there someone else?

BUDDY. No. Of course not.

JENNY. You *were* out with someone tonight, weren't you?

BUDDY. This has nothing to do with anybody else!

JENNY. Uh huh ... so we're talking about just you and me. When did you ... stop loving me?

BUDDY. Jenny, what's the difference? This isn't gonna do any good. *(He gets up and walks away from the bed.)*

JENNY. *(On the verge of tears; she follows him.)* If you stopped, you can start again. You don't just quit.

BUDDY. Nobody said we should quit.

JENNY. There's never been a divorce in my family. You don't throw twelve years of marriage away.

BUDDY. I didn't say divorce. I'm trying to be honest. You asked me.

JENNY. I gave up everything for you. Northwestern, my job.

BUDDY. Oh, God.

JENNY. We were in love *together*. I didn't chase you! What don't you like? The way I dress? I'll throw out my Laura Ashley.

BUDDY. You don't have to get rid of your dresses. *(He returns to the bed and sits. She joins him.)*

JENNY. What is it then? Buddy, we're still the same people.

BUDDY. Are we? People change.

JENNY. *No! (She kisses him passionately.)* Maybe you don't want to hear this, but I still love you.

Buddy. I know, Sweetheart. I know.

(The TELEPHONE rings.)

Jenny. My God, who could that be? *(BUDDY reacts and reaches for the phone but JENNY picks it up first.)* Hello? — Dad? *(BUDDY holds his chest, sighs in relief.)* It's late, is something wrong? — Sure, Buddy's here. *(BUDDY shakes his head "No!")* But he's sound asleep. I'll take the message. Uh huh. On the office answering machine. Go ahead. Mm hmm ... mm hmm. Okay, got it. I'll tell him in the morning, Dad. Goodnight. *(She hangs up the phone.)*
Buddy. Was it important?
Jenny. No. Just something about a radio commercial on KPRZ.
Buddy. That could be important. What was the message?
Jenny. *(She reads her note.)* They called and okayed that special weekend spot you requested.
Buddy. Really? Good.
Jenny. And they want you to know that their new signal reaches all the way to Chicago.
Buddy. That's nice.
Jenny. *(She weighs a new thought.)* Buddy ... what would you think if I change my mind and go to Chicago with you next weekend?

(BUDDY turns toward the audience. A SPOT hits his face as he reacts to his predicament. We hear a dramatic classical, music sting, as the LIGHTS dim to black.)

CURTAIN

ACT II

AT RISE: In the darkness, we hear a Thirties love song. LIGHTS up on BUDDY, sitting on a bed, in BOOTS' bedroom, in jeans and sportshirt, putting his loafers on. BOOTS, in casual "at home wear," is on the bed, her back to BUDDY, brushing her hair, reading a script.

BUDDY. *(to the audience:)* You're possibly wondering who went to Chicago? *Nobody.* A little emergency came up. One of Dad's lakes sprung a leak. And turned the model homes into model *swamps.* I spent the whole weekend with a sump pump. Boots and I laughed about it. We laughed about a lot of things.

(Widen the SPOT, to reveal BOOTS laughing as she reads the script.)

BOOTS. Your screenplay is hilarious. I love this thing Dorothy Parker says when she sees the bimbo at that high society garden party. "You can lead a horticulture, but you can't make her think."
BUDDY. Yeah. *My* favorite is George S. Kaufman's line to Groucho Marx. "The trouble with incest is that it gets you involved with relatives." *(He checks his watch.)* I've got to get out of here. My architect's gonna be waiting in my office, at seventy-five dollars an hour.

Boots. You stinker, I thought we were going to have the entire day together, so I could work on your ... jingle.

Buddy. *(dryly)* There is nothing I'd rather have you work on. *(They kiss. She touches his arm. He winces, revealing a large scrape that we hadn't seen till now.)* Ow!

Boots. Ooh, I'm sorry, I forgot. *(She looks at his wound.)* I bet that really hurts.

Buddy. I'm fine, don't worry about it.

(LIGHTS up on JENNY, across stage, in limbo. She is wearing makeup and a more attractive robe, to reflect her effort toward more physical attractiveness in Act II.)

Jenny and Boots. I am worried about it.

Jenny. I'll get some alcohol for that. *(JENNY Exits.)*

Boots. I never should have let you ride Stormy. But you were so damn convincing. You've never been on a horse before, have you?

Buddy. Of course I've been on a horse. I did very well on that one out in front of "Toys R Us."

Boots. *(looking at his scrape)* How are you going to explain this? *(She Exits.)*

Jenny. *(O.S.)* How did that happen?

Buddy. *(He calls to Jenny.)* I was checking out some rough ground and I fell.

Jenny. *(O.S. sympathetically)* Aw, honey.

(BOOTS Enters and places a vase of arranged flowers on a table.)

BOOTS. Oh God, that horrible thud when you hit the cinder path. I never should have let you ride Pete's horse without a seat belt.

BUDDY. Listen, smart ass, any mount old Pete can handle, I can handle.

BOOTS. *(dryly)* You are, of course, referring to *horses?*

BUDDY. *(overenthused, to the audience:)* Isn't that *fabulous* repartee!? We are so great together. Each of us brings out the creative talent in the other. You want to be impressed? She drew this. *(He picks up a sketch pad drawing of a giant, smiling boa constrictor, wound around a beautiful blonde. Above the drawing, printed attractively, are the words: "BUDDY THE BOA." He shows the drawing to the audience.)* She made me the lead character in her next book, "Buddy the Boa." And I'm helping her punch up the dialogue. *(He puts down the sketch pad and gestures toward BOOTS, who is arranging flowers in the vase.)* And look, she arranged these cut flowers herself. Beautiful. She doesn't care that in a few days her investment will wither and die. *Jenny* would have bought a sturdy ficus, with a reliable root system that would grow old with us.

BOOTS. *(looking at his injured arm)* You must be suffering. I'll get some ice to put on it. *(She starts to Exit. He grabs her.)*

BUDDY. You Vikings think ice is the answer to everything. Jews need warmth. *(He kisses her.)* Life giving.

BOOTS. What are you thinking?

BUDDY. I'm thinking how lucky I am. I'm thinking ... I love you. Why am I always saying that?

BOOTS. Possibly you mean it?

BUDDY. I could come up with something more original. Ira Gershwin wrote hundreds of love songs and never once said, "I love you." How about ... *(He holds her dramatically.)* "Boots, you is my woman now?" *(They laugh, then kiss.)*

(JENNY Enters, across stage, with alcohol and cotton.)

JENNY. Okay, come here.
BOOTS. I'll get your ice. *(BOOTS Exits. BUDDY crosses to JENNY's bedroom.)*
BUDDY. That's gonna hurt. I hear ice is much better. *(JENNY dabs the cotton on the scratch.)* Ow! Honey, I'm sorry I was late.
JENNY. Only a half hour. And besides, you called. What more could I ask for?
BUDDY. I brought you a little gift. I hope it's not too personal. *(He reveals a box containing a brass and porcelain faucet.)*
JENNY. *(ecstatic)* You got me a *faucet!* It's gorgeous! *(She hugs him.)* I bought *you* a little gift too. Be kind. *(She steps back a few paces, then opens her robe, quickly "flashing" a bikini, then quickly closes it.)* Thank you for your silence. Now I'm going to burn it.
BUDDY. You will not. I love it.
JENNY. My body was not made for this. There's no place to hide. Do you know how embarrassing it is to have to buy the top and bottom of a bikini as "separates." From a teenage salesgirl with cantaloupes in her bra?
BUDDY. You look wonderful.
JENNY. Well, maybe I'll wear it for sunbathing in the backyard. The squirrels need a good laugh. *(She Exits or reaches O.S. and returns with a bag and a pile of clothes.)* Do me

a favor, drop this stuff off at Council Shop on your way to work?

BUDDY. Sure. You're getting rid of your Laura Ashley? You don't have to do that.

JENNY. It's not me anymore. And remember this? *(She holds up a boring blue cotton dress.)* You called it, "Prison matron on her day off." *(She tosses the dress at him.)*

BUDDY. I was kidding.

JENNY. *(looking at some worn-out jeans)* And these jeans have to go. They're completely worn out.

BUDDY. Are you nuts? I love those. They cradle your ass like the hands of God.

JENNY. Really? Then let's get rid of 'em and let your hands do God's work. *(She faces him and puts his hands on her behind.)* You've been awfully easy to live with lately.

BUDDY. You too.

JENNY. Thanks for all the time you've been spending with the kids.

BUDDY. Hey, they're my kids too. They *are* my kids, aren't they? *(She laughs.)* I guess you noticed that I never leave my socks on the floor anymore?

JENNY. *(She nods her head.)* I noticed. And miracle number two, you even put the toilet seat down once in a while.

BUDDY. Only because I'm getting very accurate.

JENNY. Y'know something? I find terrific husbands very sexy. *(She kisses him.)*

BUDDY. Hold that thought. Unfortunately, we have to get ready for the Madonna Lakes press party.

JENNY. *(She pulls them onto the bed.)* We have time for a leisurely quicky.

BUDDY. *(He spots the script on the bed.)* My screenplay? You read it?

JENNY. Yes, this afternoon. But I want to read it again. Later.

BUDDY. You hated it.

JENNY. I did not.

BUDDY. It doesn't leap off the page, huh? Does it at least crawl off the page?

JENNY. A lot of it leaps. But it is a little glib ... and jokey.

(A SPOT hits BOOTS, in a robe, in limbo. She's reading the script, laughing.)

BOOTS. I love the way you've portrayed Dorothy Parker.

BUDDY. *(answering BOOTS)* You really think so? *(to JENNY:)* What's too jokey? You're not talking about Dorothy Parker? She was know for her humor.

BOOTS. She's a hoot with all her wisecracks.

JENNY. But she was more than a bunch of clever quotes. Didn't you tell me she went through a series of bad love affairs? And she attempted suicide twice?

BUDDY. That's true. What about the rest of it?

JENNY. I thought it was a very good first effort.

BOOTS. I love the part where George Gershwin wrote the same waltz, over and over, for four different women, just to get them into bed. *(She laughs and Exits.)*

BUDDY. *(smiling, to BOOTS:)* Yeah. *(then irritated to JENNY:)* Y'know, other people thought it was great.

JENNY. Who? I thought you weren't showing it to anyone else.

BUDDY. I showed Mike a few pages. Did you like *anything* about it?

JENNY. I like a lot. It's just... when you tell me in your own words about the light-hearted thirties, played against the threat of war in Europe, it seems so moving and important. I always get goosebumps.

BUDDY. And you get zero bumps from my script?

JENNY. It's got some wonderful things, sweetheart. I just think it can be a little realer.

BUDDY. "Realer?" What do you want, a documentary?

(BOOTS Enters. BUDDY begins to turn from JENNY to BOOTS, as in a tennis match.)

BOOTS. I wouldn't change a word. Meryl Streep would kill for the Dorothy Parker role.
JENNY. Don't be defensive. I love the story.
BOOTS. You should be so proud.
JENNY. But you should keep challenging yourself.
BOOTS. I put checkmarks by my favorite parts.
JENNY. I wrote a few suggestions in the margins.
BOOTS. It's so touching.
JENNY. It's a little facile.
BOOTS. And witty.
JENNY. And predictable.
BUDDY. Wait a minute! Enough for Christ sake!

(The SPOTLIGHT on BOOTS dims.)

JENNY. Honey, my notes are in pencil.

BUDDY. No, that's okay. I want you to be honest. *(He riffles through the script.)* A *few* suggestions? I'll look at it later. We'd better get ready. I want to check the models to make sure Dad didn't sneak crucifixes into the master bedrooms.

JENNY. I planned a little surprise for us, for after the party. *(She hands him an envelope. He opens it.)*

(The sound of a Thirties love song.)

BUDDY. A surprise? What? Tickets? "An Evening with Bobby Short! A Tribute to The Thirties." Twenty-eight dollars a ticket?

JENNY. It's only money. I don't believe I said that.

BUDDY. Dammit. Honey, I'm hosting that party. All the subcontractors will be there. I don't think I can go.

JENNY. Yes you can. Dad said it would be over by eight.

BUDDY. But I've got customers coming in at nine. What a wonderful thing to do. Dammit, I'd love to go to this. Why not take Mom? She loves that music. I'm sorry, sweetheart.

JENNY. It's okay.

BUDDY. *(to the audience:)* God, I hate all this lying. I've gotten so good at it. I don't even smile anymore. *(to JENNY:)* Sweetie, I promise, I'll make it up to you.

JENNY. I just thought you'd enjoy it.

BUDDY. Of course I would've. *(He kisses her.)* What the hell, we have a little time. *(He caresses her.)*

(LIGHTS dim on the bedroom. The MUSIC swells and ends. LIGHTS come up on the sales office, decorated for a party. We see some colorful displays with floor plans and renderings of the models with the words, "The Como," "The Lugano," "The Geneva." MOM, DAD and MIKE Enter.)

MOM. Those display homes are right out of "House Beautiful." Where did Buddy learn to decorate like that?

MIKE. Mom, I hate to tell you this.

MOM. What?

MIKE. Buddy's a faygeleh.

MOM. *(laughing)* Are you crazy?

MIKE. Dad, the houses look terrific. You'll sell all you can build.

DAD. Yeah, if I can get my foundations in before winter.

MIKE. Has Gillespie been here? He's picking up my house plans.

DAD. Gillespie's doing your foundations? That could be a problem. You're using my subs?

MIKE. A few.

DAD. A few? How few?

MIKE. Gillespie, United Lumber, Columbia Iron, Loftus Tile and Arc Electric.

DAD. That's a *few?* Who'd you leave out, the little guy who brings us bottled water? You didn't use your head, Mike.

MIKE. I've heard that often enough. In other words, I'm stupid.

DAD. I didn't say you're stupid. You're impulsive. In

January, when we're up to our ass in snow, and we each have a foundation to pour and Gillespie only has one concrete truck? Who gets it?

MOM. Then the father and the son talk to each other calmly and decide who gets it. It's concrete, not gold.

DAD. Dear, this is something you know nothing about.

MOM. *Dear,* what I've forgotten about dealing with people, you still have to learn.

MIKE. Mom, please, this is my argument, not yours.

MOM. You can have it back as soon as I stop it.

MIKE. Dad, I'm getting out of here, before we both say things we don't mean. Y'see, this is why I want my own business!

DAD. Fine, have your own business. But when you come into *my* business naked, you should go out naked!

MOM. Nobody's going anywhere naked.

MIKE. Okay Dad, I won't use any of your subs. I'll tell Gillespie to forget it. Goodnight. *(He Exits.)*

DAD. You don't have to leave the party.

MOM. Are you satisfied?

DAD. You think I enjoyed that? Look, we argued, it's over. I'll smooth it out.

MOM. You're some smoother. You smooth things like an elephant smooths an ant hill.

(BUDDY and JENNY Enter.)

BUDDY. Hi. Dad, what's with you and Mike?

MOM. What's *always* with Dad and Mike?

DAD. Maybe it's just as well that Mike left. He might think what we're doing for *Buddy,* is because of what *he* did. *(DAD pours glasses of wine.)*

BUDDY. We're doing something for Buddy?

DAD. Wait till you hear. Mother and I have a toast to make. To our new partner.

BUDDY. *What?*

DAD. That's right, not our employee, our partner. But I'll let our corporate secretary tell you. Dear?

MOM. From now on...

DAD. *(to MOM: coaching her)* Don't forget, the profits on *every* home.

MOM. I know. From now on...

DAD. Not just the *first* section.

MOM. I *know.* From now on...

DAD. A *full third.*

MOM. Will you *please?*

DAD. Right, it's your surprise.

MOM. *(to BUDDY: with sarcasm toward DAD)* Surprise, you get a full third of the profits on every home.

BUDDY. *(impressed)* A *third?*

JENNY. My God.

DAD. God doesn't get the credit for this one.

MOM. Of *course* he gets the credit. Don't joke with God!

DAD. *(holding his wine glass high)* Bona fortuna.

MOM. What happened to l'chayim?

DAD. *Drink.* And Buddy, I'm not just talking about three hundred houses.

BUDDY. What do you mean?

DAD. I have a feeling about Madonna Lakes. Almost a

religious feeling. We've got the value, the location... you did a fabulous job on the models. So, I bought another hundred and fifty acres.

BUDDY. *(shocked disbelief)* You bought another hundred and fifty acres without telling me? Dad, you know I've had these plans about being a writer.

DAD. Because of your jokes, you're not interested in a partnership?

BUDDY. No, I mean, yes, I'm interested. I just want to think it over.

DAD. *(impatiently)* He wants to *think.* Go ahead, think. I'm talking about a third of the profits on all the houses, *plus,* the *shopping center* when we build it.

BUDDY. The shopping center, too?

DAD. *(describing it expansively, with his hands)* Of course, *"Madonna Lakes Mall."* Bishop Balducci already blessed the ground for us. *(He makes the crossing sign of blessing.)*

BUDDY. *(to the audience:)* He *would* throw in the shopping center... on bless-ed ground. I'd be nuts to turn this down. It could solve a lot of problems. I could breathe a little, have my own checkbook.

(BOOTS Enters, carrying a drink.)

DAD. Miss Clark? What a nice surprise.
BUDDY. Boots?!
BOOTS. Hello. I just wanted to say congratulations.
BUDDY. I, I... didn't know you were, uh... Great! This is Boots Clark, our account exec from KPRZ. You know Dad. This is my mother, Ruth Apple.
BOOTS. Hello, Mrs. Apple.

MOM. Hello, Boots.

BUDDY. And my wife, Jenny.

JENNY. Hi, Buddy told me all about you. I love the jingle you wrote.

BOOTS. Thank you.

BUDDY. *(nervously to BOOTS:)* So, Pete couldn't come? Pete's her fiancé. He's a vice president over at Anheuser Busch. I've met him. Nice guy, *huge* guy. They ride horses together. *Huge* horses.

BOOTS. No, Pete couldn't make it. Please, don't let me interrupt. I'm just checking the displays. *(BOOTS moves to the wall displays.)*

JENNY. Well, Buddy? What's your decision?

BUDDY. *(He looks from BOOTS to JENNY.)* About what? What do you mean?

JENNY. Dad's wonderful offer!

BUDDY. *Oh!* The answer is *yes.* Thanks, Dad. You too, Mom, it's terrific.

DAD. *(He shakes BUDDY'S hand.)* Okay partner, we got a deal. *(to MOM)* And I did not talk him into it.

MOM. Did I say anything?

BUDDY. Listen, what time do you have to leave for the concert? It's almost eight.

MOM. *(She rises, puts on a sweater.)* I didn't realize the time. *(to BOOTS:)* We're going to hear Bobby Short play music by Gershwin and Cole Porter.

BOOTS. Oh yes, I love that music. You're all going?

BUDDY. No, *they're* going. I'm staying. I've got people coming in.

DAD. Who *are* these people?

BUDDY. *(to the audience:)* Yeah, who *are* these people? *(to*

DAD:) The, uh ... Delgados. Angela and Tony Delgado. You're going to be late.
  JENNY. *(She kisses BUDDY.)* I'm sorry you'll miss this.
  BUDDY. Me too. Have a wonderful time, honey. Bye, Mom. *(MOM and JENNY Exit.)*
  DAD. Don't forget to tell the Delgados about the entrance hall in the Lugano.
  BUDDY. Right, Dad.
  DAD. And the *atrium. (and DAD is gone)*
  BOOTS. Jenny's very nice.
  BUDDY. I know, didn't we agree on nine o'clock? How come you're here so early?
  BOOTS. Maybe I had to see her, I don't know.

(DAD Enters.)

  DAD. Delgado? That's definitely Italian. I could drop the ladies off and come right back.
  BUDDY. Relax, Dad, have a good time. I can handle them.
  DAD. Sure you can. If you close 'em, call me. *(DAD Exits.)*
  BOOTS. Buddy, I feel like a hit man.
  BUDDY. I know how you feel, but you shouldn't.
  BOOTS. I'm going to say something you don't want to hear.
  BUDDY. Please, don't say anything. Just listen. You knew Jenny existed before this.
  BOOTS. Buddy, it's too much for me. I'm losing respect for myself.
  BUDDY. Boots, we have something so special.

BOOTS. I don't think we should go on seeing each other.

BUDDY. But Boots... *(to the audience)* She's right. I don't blame her for dumping me. She could have anyone. What does she need with a married Jew who falls off horses?

(DAD Enters.)

DAD. Excuse me.

BUDDY. *Yes*, Dad?

DAD. Boots, is that your BMW, with the cute license plate, "HORSEY?"

BOOTS. It sure is.

DAD. You're blocking me.

BOOTS. I was just leaving anyway. Here's next week's schedule.

BUDDY. We'll talk about it soon?

BOOTS. Goodbye, Buddy.

DAD. Boots, I'll bet I could move you into a Lugano for less than you put down on your Horsey. *(BOOTS and DAD Exit.)*

BUDDY. *(suffering, to the audience:)* Oh, goddamit. How could she do this? I'm so right for her. And she's so right for me. Y'know, Gershwin was always looking for the perfect woman too. Finally, when he met Paulette Goddard, early in 1937, he fell totally in love. He asked her to marry him, but it was too late. George died a few months later. He was 38. I've got to talk to Boots and change her mind. How? *(He rubs his arm "wound.")* Infection! With the possibility of blood poisoning. *Gangrene.* And it would be her fault. The only question is, will guilt work on a gentile? *(BUDDY Exits.)*

(LIGHTS up on JENNY and BUDDY'S bedroom. MOM and JENNY, in an expensive looking, brightly colored sweater, sort laundry from a laundry basket.)

JENNY. Mom, you don't have to help me with this.

MOM. I've got nothing but time till Mike gets here with Ricky. Laura called me yesterday. She wanted to talk. Well mostly, she wanted to cry.

JENNY. It's awful. Next week would have been their thirteenth anniversary.

MOM. She said she'd take Mike back in a minute. I don't think I could do that. If someone doesn't want me once, I don't want them ten times.

JENNY. She'll need a college degree to get a decent job. And she has even fewer credits than I have.

MOM. *(She puts socks in BUDDY'S sock drawer.)* Laura's not thinking of a job, she's thinking of a husband. She's already dating.

JENNY. Uhh! The thought of dating again.

MOM. *(She finds BUDDY'S screenplay.)* Should this be in Buddy's sock drawer?

JENNY. Oh, it's his script about the thirties.

MOM. *(She finds a photo in the script.)* A picture? It's that jingle girl we met. What's her name?

JENNY. *(She takes the photo, without reacting.)* Let's see. Oh yeah, Boots. Oh good, Buddy got it for me. I'm thinking of changing my hair. I like her style.

MOM. For you? No. Laura does her hair like that. A lot of good it did her. What would be better for Laura, is if

they had talked more. Mike and Laura never talked. They either said nothing, or they argued. That's what's nice about you and Buddy, you talk.
 JENNY. We try to.
 MIKE. *(O.S.)* Hello? Anybody home?
 JENNY. We're in my bedroom, Mike. Come on back.
 MOM. *(holding up a single sock)* There's always one left over.

(MIKE Enters.)

 MIKE. Hi. Ricky took Sally and Andy out to the car.
 MOM. Oh no! the stupid alarm is on. If anyone even touches the car, it starts screaming.

(We hear a loud car ALARM O.S.)

 MOM. There it goes. I've got to stop the fool thing. Goodbye. *(MOM Exits, throwing a kiss.)*
 MIKE. *(calling O.S.)* Don't hurry, Mom. The kids love the alarm. *(He turns to JENNY.)* You look terrific. I like that sweater.
 JENNY. Thanks. But it's going back. I can't bring myself to spend a hundred and eighty dollars on a sweater.
 MIKE. Aren't you doing something different with your makeup?
 JENNY. Yeah, I went too far, didn't I?

(The car ALARM stops.)

 MIKE. No, *nice*. It's just a different look.

JENNY. I *thought* my Estee Lauder demonstrator looked too much like a hooker.

MIKE. Really, it's very effective. I'd pay as high as five hundred a night. *(She punches him playfully.)* I'm *kidding.* Actually, I'm *not.* No, I'm kidding.

JENNY. I could never be a hooker. *(judgemental, disgusted)* Guys always want to *smoke* afterwards. *(She hands MIKE a checkbook.)* Here's your checkbook. I found the mistakes and wrote a few suggestions in the margins.

MIKE. Jenny, you're fabulous. Thanks. *(He hugs her.)*

JENNY. Any time, Mike.

MIKE. *(still hugging her)* You're great.

JENNY. *(again, with a new meaning)* Any time, Mike. *(They separate.)*

MIKE. Sorry, efficiency excites me. Besides, I've been married to a woman whose checkbooks won science fiction awards. Jenny, you're a very special lady. Now that I'm separated, my eyes have been opened. You know what's out there? A lot of fucked up women.

JENNY. You mean, like Boots?

MIKE. Boots?

JENNY. Yes, you must've met Boots Clark. I found this in Buddy's drawer. *(She hands him the photo.)*

MIKE. *(smiling, the salesman)* Really? He probably forgot to take it to the office. We have photos of all the subs and suppliers for identification purposes, for deliveries.

JENNY. *(She stares, unconvinced.)* You're a wonderful brother.

MIKE. No kidding, that's very standard. I mean we're talking about Buddy, *please.* Listen, there's something I've been thinking about. At first I thought it was a bad idea because you're my sister-in-law, but I've never been rational, so why start now?

(We hear the front door close O.S.)

JENNY. Buddy's home.
MIKE. Then I'll say this fast. I *want* you. *(He smiles.)* To be my bookkeeper.
JENNY. You do?
MIKE. Yeah, it makes so much sense. You know the building business. You love figures and I can trust you.
JENNY. Oh Mike, that's *wonderful*. I accept, before you change your mind.

(She hugs him as BUDDY Enters.)

BUDDY. Hi.
MIKE. Hi, how you doing, Bud?
JENNY. Guess what? Mike wants me to be his bookkeeper, isn't that marvelous?
BUDDY. What a great idea.
MIKE. Isn't it? Well, we'll get started tomorrow, I'll call you. — Buddy?
BUDDY. Yeah?
MIKE. *(a subtle warning)* Stay loose, pal. *(MIKE crosses to the door, turns, looks at BUDDY sympathetically, Exits.)*
BUDDY. Mike is really smart. You're perfect for him.
JENNY. *(Angry, she hands the photo to BUDDY.)* Here. I found this in your sock drawer, hidden in your script! *(JENNY Exits.)*

BUDDY. *(calling JENNY O.S.)* Wait a minute. What do you mean hid ... I wasn't hiding a thing. *(to the audience: frustrated)* Shit! I knew this was gonna happen. Now I'll have to lie to her again. Why didn't I just throw the damn thing away? I'll tell you why. Because for a whole week, this was my only contact with her. *(He looks at the photo.)* Then, after my fortieth phone call, she agreed to see me.

(BUDDY moves to BOOTS' bedroom. BOOTS Enters, eating ice cream.)

BUDDY. Hi.
BOOTS. *(She looks at his arm.)* What a fake. You scared me. Some emergency. Your arm is healed.
BUDDY. Of course it is. You just touched it.
BOOTS. I should have known better with you. Want some ice cream?
BUDDY. I'd love some. *(She offers spoon, he kisses her mouth.)* Delicious.
BOOTS. Please don't do that.
BUDDY. It's your fault for having such a wonderful mouth.
BOOTS. Look, I knew your arm was okay. The only reason I let you come over is ... well, I was a little abrupt the other night.
BUDDY. A *little?* Do you have any idea how much that threw me? Today, I wrote up a thirty year loan for an eighty year old customer.
BOOTS. *(She smiles, then regains her resolve.)* I'm not going to be responsible for messing up a marriage. Ever since I

was a kid, my mother talked about my awful stepmother, Christine, the homewrecking bitch.

BUDDY. *(He looks at a framed picture.)* Is this the bitch with your father? She's gorgeous. Boy, was he human.

BOOTS. No, that's my mother, about twenty years ago. I'm trying to tell you something important.

BUDDY. Sure, go ahead. — Your *Mother?!* The same lady I met?

BOOTS. Yes, before she gained seventy pounds after Daddy left. Revenge eating.

BUDDY. She sure showed *him*.

BOOTS. Buddy, I love your humor. And you're so damn smart and creative. We've had a wonderful time together, but it's over. I'm in love with Pete and I'm sure you love Jenny. And besides that, I'm moving to New York.

BUDDY. New York?!

BOOTS. Yes, I've been offered a job with a larger station there.

BUDDY. Wow! When did all this happen?

BOOTS. A few days ago. I'm leaving tomorrow. *(He reacts.)* It's just an initial meeting, to see if they like me and I like them. I wouldn't move till next month.

BUDDY. That doesn't give me much time.

BOOTS. You're not going to talk me out of it.

BUDDY. You're right. You should do what's best for you and I'm going to do the same.

BOOTS. What's that supposed to mean?

BUDDY. I'm going to ask Jenny for a divorce. It's time.

BOOTS. Buddy.

BUDDY. This has nothing to do with you. Well, okay, *something*. But it would have happened anyway.

BOOTS. You're not going to leave Jenny. And you shouldn't.

BUDDY. I can't help it. I don't want to spend the rest of my life feeling lonely. So anyway, I'm going home... and talk to her.

BOOTS. You've never told me you wanted to end your marriage before.

BUDDY. I know. I didn't want to bullshit you. I guess I wasn't ready to leave before. Now I am.

BOOTS. You're sure you really want to do this?

BUDDY. I'm sure.

BOOTS. Oh, God.

BUDDY. I'm doing this for me, okay?

BOOTS. *(emotionally)* It wasn't easy for me to say goodbye. I love you very much. *(She kisses him, then Exits.)*

(JENNY Enters from behind BUDDY. LIGHTS dim on BOOTS' bedroom.)

JENNY. I want to know what going on between you and Boots?

BUDDY. *Nothing.* I took her photograph. She wanted to give one to her boyfriend and she didn't have a camera.

JENNY. Really?

BUDDY. *Pete,* remember? I forgot to give it to her.

JENNY. I'd love to believe that. But I don't. And you could've picked a better day for this shit. Andy got thrown out of nursery school today.

BUDDY. After six weeks? They can't do that.
JENNY. Well they did it.
BUDDY. Why? What the hell did he do?
JENNY. He hit another child with a swing and they said he did it on purpose.
BUDDY. He's *four*, for Christ sake!
JENNY. The little girl's mother was hysterical and I don't blame her.
BUDDY. Screw 'em. We'll find another school. I'll help you look.
JENNY. That's alright, I'll handle it. But I can only deal with one crisis at a time. And I can't handle you right now.
BUDDY. What does that mean?
JENNY. I'm not gonna put up with this. It's worse than not having you. *(She looks at the photo.)* This explains everything. Late hours, late movies, your endless search for new acreage.
BUDDY. That photo isn't for me. You can ask her.
JENNY. No! I refuse to be a goddam detective. I'm not going to live this way. I'm tired of trying to figure out what the hell's wrong with me. There isn't a damn thing wrong with me. And there's plenty wrong with you!
BUDDY. Jenny ... *(He reaches out to her, she pulls back.)*
JENNY. Get away, Buddy. Don't touch me. All those wonderful feelings I've had for you lately are gone.
BUDDY. Honey...
JENNY. I think you'd better get out of here.
BUDDY. You know you don't want me to leave.
JENNY. Don't tell me what I want! I don't want to be lied to anymore. Please, just get the hell out of here!

BUDDY. Whatever you say.

(LIGHTS dim on JENNY. BUDDY turns to the audience, totally undone by her anger.)

BUDDY. Jesus Christ. — I hope you don't mind if we don't talk?

(BUDDY moves to the darkened Sales Office, and lies down on the couch, as we hear a love song from the Thirties." LIGHTS up on DAD, in limbo, on the telephone.)

DAD. *(into the phone)* Jenny? Hi. I never have to worry about waking *you* up when I call early. Wake that bum, Buddy, for me, will ya? — He's gone already? At seven A.M.? where? You don't? Maybe he's still trying to close that Delgado deal. Don't worry about it. I'll track him down. Bye, Jenny.

(The SPOT on DAD dims. Dawn LIGHTS the Sales Office. MIKE Enters, with an empty canvas bag. He flips the LIGHT on.)

MIKE. Buddy, are you here?
BUDDY. *(He rises, rubs eyes.)* Yeah, just taking a little snooze. I was checking some sale figures. How come you're here so early?
MIKE. *(Cleans desk into canvas bag.)* Just gathering the last of my things, before I ride off into the sunset. Hey, want to catch the Cardinal game?
BUDDY. I can't, Dad called. He's coming out to have

one of his meetings.

MIKE. On Sunday morning? What about?

BUDDY. We're have a small voodoo ceremony. We've got this little "Mike doll." We'll be sticking pins up your ass.

MIKE. *(He chuckles.)* How's Boots?

BUDDY. Wonderful. What's in the box?

MIKE. Oh, it's a new beeperless answering machine. Here, would you ask Jenny to hook this up in your basement by Monday? I've got the phone company putting in an extra line. *(He tosses BUDDY the box.)*

BUDDY. In my basement?

MIKE. Yeah. I figure Jenny could hook up the computer down there and I'll have a temporary office.

BUDDY. You're gonna be in my basement, all day, every day? You and Jenny?

MIKE. Yeah, going over bids ... making projections.

BUDDY. Making projections? Now that I get the whole picture, I'm not crazy about it. *(He tosses MIKE the box.)*

MIKE. In other words, you don't trust me?

BUDDY. Let's say I kind of half trust you, from the waist up. *(His hand indicates from his waist up.)* You shouldn't've told me about Lot Eighty-Three.

MIKE. How can you even compare Jenny to Eighty-Three? Jenny's not gonna hop in the sack with her brother-in-law. Even if it *is* me. She's so innocent, so devoted, so intelligent. *(He tosses the box to BUDDY.)*

BUDDY. *(He avoids the toss, the box hits the floor.)* Stay the hell out of my basement!

MIKE. What is it with you? A few months ago, you were

looking for some kind of divorce button to push.

BUDDY. Well *you're* not the button!

MIKE. Who says I'm trying to be? I'm just curious to know when you're gonna make a decision?

BUDDY. I don't know.

MIKE. You damn well better think about it. You're not being fair to either Jenny or Boots or *you*. You gotta walk away from one of 'em. I could flip a coin for you.

BUDDY. Will you leave me alone? You always do this to me, goddamit! "Have you finished with your chicken? Are you gonna eat your spaghetti?" You're like a vulture. Stop circling me!

MIKE. That's the thanks I get? Let me tell you something, pal. Everyone might not think I'm a great son, but I'm one helluva brother. I ever do anything to disprove that?

BUDDY. No. Not yet.

MIKE. Okay, now I know you slept here last night.

BUDDY. How?

MIKE. Jenny told me, when we woke up together this morning. *Putz,* I saw your car here, at two thirty A.M. Lot Eighty-Three and I had a little six-month anniversary party.

BUDDY. Yeah, I slept here. Jenny really flipped.

MIKE. That photo of Boots, huh? *(totally losing patience)* You are a real remedial student. You *never* take pictures of 'em! You commit their bodies to memory! The shit really hit the fan, huh?

BUDDY. Every blade.

MIKE. You've got to make a decision, Bud.

(DAD Enters from a back office.)

DAD. Good morning.
MIKE. Dad? Where'd you come from?
DAD. I parked in back.
MIKE. I was just leaving. I've got to meet some subs. None of yours. *(He picks up the box.)*
DAD. Stay a minute. I was going to call you. Listen, forget what I said about not using my subs. Use 'em, all of 'em, including Gillespie.
MIKE. Thanks, Dad, but I'm not taking a chance on holding you up.
DAD. Take the chance, I insist.
MIKE. You're just doing this to be nice.
DAD. When I'm being nice, I'll tell you. I made a deal.
MIKE. A deal?
DAD. Yeah, I called all the subs and convinced 'em to give both of us an additional ten percent off, for the extra business they'll get from our *two* subdivions.
MIKE. *(a mixture of amusement and frustration)* Right, terrific. Jesus Christ, even when I *leave*, I don't really *leave*. *(MIKE Exits.)*
DAD. *(calling O.S.)* Glad you like the deal. *(to BUDDY:)* Okay, Buddy, let's talk.
BUDDY. Dad, I really don't have time right now.
DAD. This is important, it won't take long, sit down.
BUDDY. Alright, what's it about?
DAD. My medical building at Six Hundred Washington. Remember when I bought that building, how I

was in love with it? It was new, it was gorgeous.

BUDDY. Yeah. It's a terrific building.

DAD. It *was,* seven years ago. Now it's a piece of shit. Twenty-eight percent vacant.

BUDDY. Twenty eight? My God.

DAD. It's not even carrying the loan. The location's not good enough for my goddam doctors anymore. They're moving out like gypsies. To make things worse, that warehouse I sold to buy the medical building is worth three times what I got for it. I gave it away.

BUDDY. You never told me that.

DAD. When you're a shmuck, why advertise? Every time I drive by that warehouse, my stomach makes its opening remarks. "Hey, Norman, *idiot!* You really blew *that* one." Bud, I don't want that to happen to you.

BUDDY. No problem. I can't afford any buildings.

DAD. I'm talking about Boots, *your* medical building.

BUDDY. What?!

DAD. And *Jenny,* your warehouse.

BUDDY. *Dad,* what is this? You're kidding me?

DAD. Buddy, I'm not blind. I make mistakes on buildings, not people.

BUDDY. *(He smiles his old lying smile.)* It's really funny that you think there's something going on between us. *(DAD stares accusingly.)* Okay, there's something going on. I'm glad I told you. I'm in love with Boots.

DAD. Nice. It sounds like a *foot fetish. (He rises, frustrated.)* Very smart, Buddy. that's all we need at Madonna Lakes. A *sin.* Look, I know Boots is a beautiful girl. But you don't throw everything away for that.

BUDDY. She's more than beauitful, she's intelligent

and witty and sensitive.

DAD. You wouldn't think of leaving Jenny? That's out of the question. Jenny's a wonderful girl. She's got a head on her shoulders and she's pretty. Okay, so she's not gigantic up here. *(He touches his chest.)*

BUDDY. That doesn't mean a thing.

DAD. What is it with my sons? Neither of them will make a goddam commitment. If things aren't working exactly right, they throw their hands up and walk.

BUDDY. I'm not throwing my hands up. I've thought about this a long time. The truth is I probably never should have married Jenny.

DAD. Then why did you?

BUDDY. *(to the audience.)* He can ask me that?! *(to DAD:)* Because you talked me into it!

DAD. You're nuts.

BUDDY. You don't remember telling me that I could lose Jenny to a football hero at Northwestern? You don't remember dangling ten thousand dollars in front of my face?

DAD. Okay, it's vaguely familiar. No wonder you don't think your marriage is working. From the beginning, you had one foot out the door. A marriage can't work unless you put your ass on the line. You've got to say, I've closed the deal on this woman. There's no "out clause." So, she needs a few improvements? A rebuilt staircase, a hotter furnace? *Put 'em in!*

BUDDY. Dad, Jenny is my wife, not my fixer-upper!

DAD. The hell she isn't! And you're *hers!* Like your mother and me. Two partners who count on each other, who *own* each other. Weren't you watching us all these years? Didn't you learn anything about loyalty?

BUDDY. I know you have a good marriage, but that doesn't mean it's the same...

DAD. *(interrupting)* Yeah, don't forget what you wanted to say.

BUDDY. *No!* I want to say it, *now!*

(MOM Enters, carrying a knitting bag.)

MOM. You can both wait! *I've* got things to say!

BUDDY. Mom! *(to DAD:)* You were hiding her in your office?

MOM. Nobody hides me. I happened to be back there, knitting.

DAD. That's right. Wherever I go, she goes. We're partners.

MOM. *Dear!* I don't want to hear anymore about partners. You can go to hell with your partnership! And loyalty you can get from a poodle!

DAD. You're anrgy with *me?* You don't think I gave him good advice?

MOM. It was wonderful advice. Try *taking* it sometime. I was back there dropping stitches from listening to you talk about our wonderful marriage. We *own* each other. What do *I* own? The pots and the pans and the housework?

DAD. How can you say that? You own half of everything, including *me*. And when I go, you get it all.

MOM. God forbid! I don't what it all when you're dead! I want us to live now. I'm tired of doing everything the way *you* want. We *go* where *you* want. I mean we *don't* go, because you're always working. *(to BUDDY:)* Last year I had to cancel our "TWA Getaway" *twice.*

DAD. You're forgetting, I was building you a new house.

MOM. I didn't need a new house. I like my old house, with a full basement, instead of on freezing concrete, where I feel like my feet never left Russia.

DAD. Slab construction happens to be the newest and the finest.

MOM. And the *oldest*. I'll be on a slab soon enough, don't *rush me! (to BUDDY:)* And that car he bought me. I needed a Mercedes? I never wanted a Mercedes. I don't forgive and forget so easy.

DAD. *(to BUDDY:)* Will you tell your mother that the Mercedes is the safest car made?

MOM. *(getting increasingly upset)* Safe? Every time I drive it I've got to worry if a crook will steal the radio that's *so* wonderful *I don't know how to work it!*

BUDDY. Mom, calm down, your side's gonna start hurting.

MOM. My side hurts when I *get* aggravation. This time I'm *giving.* I left Russia to run away from Stalin and I end up *married* to him.

DAD. So, maybe I'm headstrong, but you know I love you.

MOM. Love *is* what love *does.* It's more than jokes and gooses.

DAD. Alright, you're not totally wrong. But while you're angry, save some for your son. Tell him, he's going to ruin his life.

MOM. As much as I love Jenny, and I know how perfect she is for him, *no*. I'm not giving anyone advice. I'm not saying I approve what's going on with him and this Boots. It's *killing* me. *(to BUDDY:)* Not that it should influence you. *(to DAD:)* You think I've never felt like walking out? Plenty of times, believe me.

DAD. The point is, you *didn't.*

MOM. *Yet!* It's Buddy's life, he should make his own decision, even if it's stupid. He knows what we want, but whatever he decides, *(the martyr)* We'll live with it.

BUDDY. Thanks, Mom. *(He kisses MOM.)*

MOM. But make a decision *now*. With one rear end, you can't sit on two chairs. *(to DAD:)* Let's go ... "*partner.*"

DAD. In a minute.

MOM. See that it's a minute! I'll be outside ... waiting in my safe Mercedes ... which tomorrow, I am trading in for a *Chevrolet! (MOM Exits.)*

DAD. *(to BUDDY: accusingly)* I *hope* you're *happy!* She is not a woman who explodes. Except when her son is playing around.

BUDDY. Dad, I'm not playing around. I know you love Jenny, but this time I've got to think about what's right for me. Because I'm going to live with my decision for a long time. *(He checks his watch, starts to Exit.)* Now if you'll excuse me, I've got to meet someone.

DAD. Just so you know, that partnership I offered you was meant for you *and* your family. *(BUDDY stops.)*

BUDDY. In other words, no marriage, no partnership? Clever. And if that doesn't scare me enough, no marriage, no *job?*

DAD. I didn't say that. What I'm saying is, a guy I'd

want as my partner, to get *fifty percent* of Madonna Lakes Estates...

BUDDY. *Fifty* percent?

DAD. That's right, I was just coming to that part. I've decided to make you an equal partner. And for that, I want a mensch.

BUDDY. If you can't close the deal, raise the stakes. Brilliant! No deal this time, Dad. I quit! *(He starts to Exit.)*

DAD. And I thought Mike was the stubborn one. You're only quitting because you know I'm right about Jenny.

BUDDY. It doesn't matter if you're wrong or right. What I do with my life is *my* decision. You're always telling me to be a mensch. How do you get to be a mensch when someone else decides everything for you? Dad, I'm not a kid. Stop treating me like one!

DAD. That's hard. Ask me something easy. You'll always be my kid. I never want to change that.

BUDDY. I don't either. I love being your kid. But Dad, as long as I can remember, I've resented you.

DAD. You'll get over it.

BUDDY. No I won't. Remember when I wanted that Yogi Berra catcher's mitt for little league? And you told me, "Smart money doesn't buy a catcher's mitt. What if you don't get picked as catcher? Then you're stuck with a large leather paperweight."

DAD. I don't remember that, but that sounds like a smart man talking.

BUDDY. Of course. So you bought me a fielder's glove. And I didn't get picked as catcher. Because every time

Larry Gordon burned one in, my hand stung all the way up to my armpit. Dad, I wanted to be a goddamn catcher. I wouldn't have minded being stuck with that catcher's mitt. You should have just ... It was important to me.

DAD. You're right. I'll buy you a catcher's mitt. *(BUDDY reacts.)* Okay, I admit, I like having control. But we don't always get what we like. So, from now on, if we can't decide on something together, we'll flip a coin, we'll arm wrestle.

BUDDY. Dad, I don't want to be a builder. I want to write.

DAD. Fine, write for awhile. We're just rough grading now anyway. I'll leave the door open for you.

BUDDY. Do me a favor, slam the door.

DAD. Tell me something, while you're doing this writing, what are you going to live on?

BUDDY. I've got some savings.

DAD. Buddy, how can you even *think* like that? Smart money *never* lives on capital. *(realizing)* There I go, giving you advice again. Okay, you've gotta do this? Do it. But remember, "Mr. Catcher," just in case... *(almost overcome by emotion)* I'm your backstop.

BUDDY. Thanks, Dad. *(They embrace.)*

(A Mercedes HORN honks.)

DAD. I'd better go out and make peace with your mother. *(He starts to Exit, then turns.)* Y'know, I've got to hand it to you, you've got determination. Any guy that can walk away from the deal I'm offering you, *seventy-five percent* of Madonna Lakes Estates.

BUDDY. *Dad!*
DAD. Hey, I'm allowed to joke too. Where do you think *you* got it? *(DAD Exits.)*
BUDDY. *(to the audience:)* I don't believe it, I'm free. I feel as if a great burden has been removed from me. Also, a great deal of cash. Finally, I'm ready to make the big decisions in my life. Dad said, "Go." Jenny said, "Go ... to *hell*." I can take any road I choose, do anything I want. So, I drove Boots to the airport, feeling relaxed, all my options open. No guilt, no pressure. Just that beautiful, undemanding face.

(LIGHTS up on BOOTS at the Airport Lounge. BUDDY crosses to her.)

BOOTS. Did you talk to Jenny?
BUDDY. Uh ... I know I told you I was going to, but I couldn't last night. She had a really tough day. Andy got expelled from nursery school.
BOOTS. I'm sorry. It's not that I'm pressuring you. It's just that my plans have changed.
BUDDY. How?
BOOTS. I've decided not to take that job in New York.
BUDDY. But you're flying out of here in a few minutes.
BOOTS. For a free weekend in Manhattan. I'll hit Bloomingdales, see some theatre. Then I'll meet with CBS, thank them for the offer and turn it down. Too much that matters to me is in St. Louis. My horses, my mom, you. Not in that order of importance. You *do*

intend talking to Jenny, eventually?

BUDDY. Of course. You're angry?

BOOTS. No, it must be very difficult for you. It's not something you can just do on cue. And you certainly didn't.

BUDDY. You have no idea what I'm dealing with. She absolutely panics at the thought of being without me. Which is silly, because she's got so much going for her now. Try to convince *her* of that. She'd probably have a nervous breakdown if I left.

(LIGHTS up on JENNY, in a LIMBO FANTASY SETTING. She's lovely in a long black gown.)

JENNY. *(laughing)* A breakdown? Buddy, you are so full of it.

BUDDY. My God, is that *you?* It couldn't be.

JENNY. Of course it's me. Don't you recognize your "warehouse?" Just the way you wanted me. Wholesome, sexy ... And list free.

BUDDY. *(to the audience:)* I know she's at home with the kids. I'm having hallucinations. This is how Vinnie Van Go went nuts.

BOOTS. Jenny'll do fine without you. Women are much stronger than men realize.

BUDDY. Yeah, I know. *(to JENNY:)* You look fabulous.

JENNY. Thank you. You sure know how to improve a fixer-upper. I just wanted to wish you good luck. I hope you enjoy your freedom.

BUDDY. My freedom?

JENNY. If you don't want me *once,* I don't want you *ten* times.
BUDDY. I didn't want you the way you *were.*
JENNY. That's tough. Bye.
BOOTS. I'd better check on my flight.
BUDDY. *(to BOOTS: quickly)* Good idea. *(BOOTS Exits, JENNY starts to leave.)* Jenny, *wait!* There's never been a divorce in your family.
JENNY. Buddy, don't fall apart. People change, they move on.
BUDDY. *(a sudden realization)* There's someone *else,* isn't there?

(MIKE Enters in a tux, with a red rural pocket kerchief, a bowtie and construction boots.)

MIKE. We'd better get going, Babe.
BUDDY. *Mike?* what are *you* doing here?
MIKE. *(a smiling wave of recognition)* Hi, I'm part of your hallucination. Thanks for including me. *(He puts his arm around JENNY.)*
BUDDY. You mind taking your hands off my wife?!
MIKE. You mean your ex-wife. Jen and I are married now.
BUDDY. *What?!*
JENNY. Smartest move I ever made. I didn't even have to change my monograms. We're off to Chicago. We've been named "1990 Builders of the Year."
MIKE. We're *partners.* In business *and* in life. Jen handles the office, I handle the field. *(He puts his arm around JENNY.)*

BUDDY. Well, just stop handling *Jenny,* dammit!

MIKE. Bud, we're brothers. I don't want this to hurt that. But you were obviously through with Jenny. And you know how I love your leftovers. *(to JENNY:)* Sweetheart, wind this up. First class is boarding. *(MIKE Exits.)*

JENNY. *(to MIKE: O.S.)* Be right there, darling. Buddy, thanks for a great twelve years. Especially that last couple of months. You forced me out of my shell and made me feel really good about myself.

BUDDY. Right, I did that, don't forget.

(BOOTS Enters.)

BOOTS. My plane's on schedule. Maybe while I'm in New York, you'll make up your mind. You're the one who said you wanted a divorce. Now it seems like you're waffling.

JENNY. Bye, Buddy. You've been a total jerk.

BUDDY. I know, but I was confused.

BOOTS. And unreliable.

JENNY. And a liar and a cheat. *(JENNY Exits.)*

BUDDY. *(confused and frustrated)* Hold it! Boots, I don't have to wait till you get back from New York. I've made my decision.

BOOTS. You have?

BUDDY. Yes. Listen, I know what I said last night, and I meant it. Y'see, the problem is...

BOOTS. I knew it. I deserve this. Buddy, don't bother. I went over every possible excuse last night. What is it, you can't leave because you love your kids too much?

BUDDY. You're right, the kids are so young and to just walk away from them now would be ... *(He shakes his head.)* No, I want to be totally honest, I didn't get as far as the kids. It's Jenny.

BOOTS. You really think she'd be suicidal?

BUDDY. It's not that. It's the way I've started to feel about her. I think I'm ... God, this is tough.

BOOTS. You're in *love* with her!

BUDDY. Yeah.

BOOTS. I don't know what to say. I'm speechless.

BUDDY. But when I told you I loved you, I'm sure I meant it. And I still have so much affection for you. Boots, if there were two of me, one of us would definitely be marrying you.

BOOTS. Buddy, *please,* don't try to make me feel better. For one thing, you're lousy at it. And for another thing, you've got a lot of goddam nerve, pushing yourself into my life with your jokes and your interesting talk and your total devotion. You *made* me fall in love with you, you bastard!

BUDDY. It wasn't a plot. I felt so close to you. I still *do.*

BOOTS. But you *never* loved me. You just put me on a pedestal. And even then, you hadn't decided whether I really belonged up there. You were always judging me.

BUDDY. I have never judged you, *ever.*

BOOTS. *Bullshit,* Buddy. Gentiles can be sensitive too. You know how you've always complimented me on how flat my stomach is?

BUDDY. *(He nods.)* It's like a slab of marble.

BOOTS. Only because I've been sucking it in! I don't want to have to live up to marble! Every time you touched me, I knew I was under inspection. My stomach! My thighs!

BUDDY. Boots, you're dreaming these things.

BOOTS. Am I?

BUDDY. *(to the audience:)* No, she's *not.* I have been judging her. Her thighs, her binge eating, her *mother.* Her ankles aren't as thin as Jenny's. And her head, forgive me, is a little too big for her body. *(He puts his hands over her head. She is unaware.)* It's kinda like a small basketball. *(to the audience: innocently)* Am I being too critical here?

BOOTS. You know what infuriated me the *most?*

BUDDY. Something we covered or something new?

BOOTS. You were never possesive enough.

BUDDY. That's *bad?*

BOOTS. You never questioned whether I was sleeping with Pete, or anybody else I dated.

BUDDY. Well I *hoped* you weren't, but I didn't feel I had the right...

BOOTS. *(She rises angrily.)* Well, I *wasn't!* And I wasn't offered that New York job because of my looks. I'm just damn *good! (He gets his wallet out.)* Put your money away! This was a business meeting. *(getting rid of some final anger)* By the way, I'm turning your account over to someone who is *short, fat* and *bitchy!* Jenny will *love* him! *(BOOTS Exits.)*

BUDDY. *(to the audience:)* Boy, has *she* changed. *(thoughtfully)* Wait a minute. I'd better think about this. I've got the two women I care most about furious at me.

It's this constant judging I've been doing. It's crazy. And it doesn't work. If Boots isn't perfect, who the hell is? *(He thinks, then nods his head.)* Jenny is. For *me,* anyway. *(He reaches O.S. and grabs a florist's box.)* I'd better get home. Jenny knows how to change the locks. What I need is a convincing excuse that she'll buy. — No, goddamit! I don't want her to buy *anything.* Why don't I just *go home?*

(BUDDY walks through limbo to JENNY'S bedroom. JENNY, in robe, with two curlers in her hair, Enters, carrying some rolls of toilet paper.)

BUDDY. Hi.

JENNY. *(She jumps, startled.)* My *God!* You scared me. You're home.

BUDDY. Of course I'm home. It's where my socks are. It's where *you* are. I brought you some flowers. *(He hands her the florist's box.)*

JENNY. From the airport?

BUDDY. The airport?

JENNY. Boots called. You forgot to get her makeup case out of your car.

BUDDY. I did? *(frustrated, to the audience:)* Shit. *(to JENNY:)* Yeah, I guess I did.

JENNY. She wants you to take it to KPRZ, so they can pouch it to New York. Evidently, she needs *paint.*

BUDDY. *Well,* I've got to get out of these clothes that I slept in last night, on the couch, in the office. You can ask Dad.

JENNY. Buddy, I want a straight answer. Have you been having an affair?

BUDDY. Jenny, I don't want to lie to you. And I don't want to lose you.

JENNY. Uh huh. And I'm supposed to live with that?

BUDDY. Honey ... I made an awful mistake.

JENNY. And you think by admitting your mistake and bringing me flowers, everything'll be okay?

BUDDY. Of course not. Here's the receipt. *(He hands her a receipt. She stares a beat, then puts it in her robe pocket.)* Jenny, I'm not the same guy you kicked out last night. I've been an idiot, coming home night after night, from a job I didn't want to be doing, expecting you to make my life wonderful. Blaming you when it wasn't.

JENNY. Buddy, there's something you'd better know. I've discovered that I could get along without you, if that's what has to be.

BUDDY. It *doesn't* have to be. You've got to believe me.

JENNY. Why the hell should I believe you, after what's happened?

BUDDY. Because somebody's gotta do something smart around here. And you've always been the best at that.

JENNY. Well I'm tired of being the best at that. And I'm tired of turning myself inside-out for you. There are things about me that are not going to change. For one thing, I'm overorganized and for another thing, I'm a *pennypincher.*

BUDDY. No, I see you as sensibly frugal.

JENNY. No, I'm *cheap*. Buddy, I don't think I'm perfect enough for you. I know how it eats at you when you can't get the raisins *inside* the little bisquits.

BUDDY. You're more than perfect enough. It just took me a while to see that. My problem was, I had this kid's dream of falling for some kind of a golden girl. But you've become that girl. And there's one other thing. I never told you this, but Dad kind of talked me into our marriage.

JENNY. He talked *you* into it *too?*

BUDDY. He talked *you* into it?

JENNY. *(She nods.)* He said you had a wonderful future in the building business. And that you were smart, sensitive and that you'd probably grow a little taller.

BUDDY. That son of a bitch.

JENNY. *You're* the son of a bitch.

BUDDY. Not anymore. You're everything I want. I love that we have a history together, and that you see right through me. And I'm insanely jealous over you. And I love the way you look ... even in curlers.

JENNY. *(She feels her hair, touches her curlers.)* Oh *no!* My God, I'm a toad! Why did I start reading that damn script? *(She removes curlers, brushes out her hair.)*

BUDDY. You read the second draft?

JENNY. Yes. I thought it might be a good idea, after Dad called and told me you quit.

BUDDY. *(to the audience: frustrated)* The *speed* of that man's *mouth.*

JENNY. If you want to know, it made me mad as hell.//
BUDDY. What can you do? That's Dad.
JENNY. At *you!* How could you give up a *partnership* without discussing it with me?
BUDDY. *(irritated)* How could I discuss it with you? It just came up. I had to quit, so I quit! It was my decision.
JENNY. It was not *your* decision. It was *our* decision. We're supposed to be in this together you know!
BUDDY. I should tell Dad to put the veins back in his neck, while I telephone my wife for instrucitons?!
JENNY. That's *right!*
BUDDY. *Bullshit!*
JENNY. Well *bullshit* to *you!* I want to be consulted when the security of this family is involved!
BUDDY. There you go again, worrying about *money!*
JENNY. Don't you *dare* accuse me of being cheap! *(She throws a roll of toilet paper and hits him.)*
BUDDY. Look, why don't you say what's really on your mind? You don't think I'm worth a shit as a writer!
JENNY. *(She shoves him onto the bed.)* You are *too!* I loved your goddam screenplay! *(She softens.)* Buddy, you're a really good writer.
BUDDY. Thanks. And thanks for those suggestions you wrote in the margins.
JENNY. My God, I threw toilet paper at you.
BUDDY. Hey, I deserved it.
JENNY. I *know.* We actually had a *fight.*

BUDDY. I'm sorry.

JENNY. No. It was a wonderful fight. I didn't cry. And I wasn't afraid you'd walk out on me.

BUDDY. I could never walk out on you. I'd miss you too much. Jenny, you're looking at the world's greatest husband ... in *training*, with a learner's permit. You want proof? I'll go out and vote right now. *Taxi!* *(He fakes an Exit. JENNY laughs.)* God, I love your laugh. But I don't want to make you laugh right now. I know what I've put you through. I've been so damn stupid and insensitive and irresponsible and selfish.

JENNY. Good, you made a list.

BUDDY. *(near tears)* Jenny, will you forgive me? It doesn't have to be all at once. *Please?*

JENNY. You know me. I never *could* throw anything away. *(They kiss.)*

(We hear a Thirties love song.)

BUDDY. Care to dance?

JENNY. *You* want to dance?

BUDDY. I'm willing to learn, if you're willing to teach me.

JENNY. I'd love to teach you to dance.

BUDDY. I hope you don't mind turning only to the left.

JENNY. Counterclockwise is my favorite direction. *(They dance. They kiss.)*

CURTAIN

PROPS

ACT I
Note: Furniture, including plants, wall decor, etc. in all scenes will be minimal and representational. In many cases, furniture and accessories can double in other scenes and locales.

BUDDY AND JENNY'S BEDROOM
A double bed or two small side-by-side beds, two night stands, with two small lamps, small dresser, a dressing table (with mirror), a stool or chair.

PROPS ON BUDDY'S BED TABLE
Pencil holder with pencils and pens
Clock radio

PROPS ON JENNY'S BED TABLE
Note pad
Telephone
Book
Speech for Mother and Daddy's anniversary party

PROPS ON BED
Pillows, bedspread, linens, pillowcases, sheets
Portable typewriter (electric or manual)
Clean and typed-on typing paper

PROPS ON FLOOR
Typing paper, socks, undershorts

PROPS ON JENNY'S VANITY
Pearls, earrings, watch, hair brush
Perfume and cosmetic bottles
Framed photo of Mother and Daddy

OTHER PROPS
Lamps and plants where needed
Letter sweater (in dresser)
Buddy's briefcase
Breakfast tray with cereal, raisins, bruised peach
Buddy's coins, wallet, keys
Jenny's sample ballot, note pad with lists, organ donor paper and pen

SALES OFFICE
A couch, a desk or flat table, small dresser or chest, a few chairs

MASONITE SIGNS
"Apple Construction Presents Heather Highlands (Plaid decor with picture of a Scots figure)
"Apple Construction Presents Madonna Lakes Estates" (Picture of a lake with Madonna and Child in the center)

LARGE DISPLAY CARD
One large card with two or three house drawings, along with the names "The Lugano," "The Como," and "The Geneva," along with dark contrasty floor plans and blocks of descriptive copy on a brightly colored board.

OTHER PROPS
Easels (if needed) for signs and/or display card
Rolled up blueprints for Mike
Mike's "Stanley" type 25' steel measuring tape
Mike's pencil and pad
Boots' briefcase and date book
Buddy's briefcase (seen in bedroom)

MOM AND DAD'S DINING ROOM
A rectangular dining table (Possibly achieved by placing an already clothed table-top on top of castered pedestal table used in restaurant scenes, to be moved by actors or stage hands)

DINNER PROPS AND FOOD
Dishes, glasses, silverware for four
Bottle of white wine
4 wine glasses
Large bowl of salad
Large bowl of noodles
Basket of bread and/or rolls
Platter of stuffed green peppers
Jenny's newspaper article on "mouth cancer"
Mom's kitchen towel and oven mittens
Dad's cigar
Jenny's swimsuit in plastic shopping bag

"THE FIRESIDE" RESTAURANT SCENES
Small pedestal table, two chairs, optional potted plant and wall treatment

104 ALMOST PERFECT

LUNCH PROPS
Salt and pepper shakers, napkin holder, ketchup bottle, 2 Budweiser bottles, empty plates, crumpled paper napkins

DINNER PROPS
Two wine glasses, mini restaurant type, table lamp

PROPS TO BE USED "IN LIMBO"
Buddy's socks with horses on them
Jenny's telephone

ACT II

BOOT'S BEDROOM
A bed, bed table or tables, dresser, dressing table. (This might be achieved by moving half of castered bed from Jenny's bedroom)

PROPS ON BOOTS' BED, BED TABLE OR DRESSING TABLE
Script, hair brush
Small vase with flowers, photo of parents
Basket of necklaces, jewelry box
Buddy the Boa drawing pad
Vase with flowers and extra flowers

JENNY'S BEDROOM

PROPS IN DRESSER DRAWER
Script with Boots' photo stuck in pages

OTHER PROPS
Bottle of alcohol and cotton swab
New bathroom faucet in transparent box
Theatre tickets (Bobby Short Concert) in small envelope
Buddy's screenplay script
Large bag for clothes for Council Shop
Laura Ashley dress
Plain blue or gray dress ("Prison matron on her day off")
Worn-out jeans

SALES OFFICE
Festive decorations for party
Model home display cards
Wine bottle and glasses
Boots' KPRZ schedule in envelope

JENNY'S BEDROOM
Plastic clothes basket with kids' clothes including socks
Mike's checkbook

BOOTS' BEDROOM
A pint container of Hagen-Daaz ice cream with spoon

SALES OFFICE
MIKE'S PROPS
New answering machine carton (weighted)
Empty canvas bag
Dopp kit, with razor, vitamins
Mom's knitting bag

AIRPORT LOUNGE
Two chairs, small low table, appropriate wall treatment. (If necessary, this could br the same as restaurant set with only a change in table top and/or wall treatment)

2 highball glasses, bowl of peanuts
Boots' large travel purse
Airline ticket, bar check

JENNY'S BEDROOM
Long flower box
3 rolls of toilet paper
2 hair rollers

PROPS TO BE USED IN LIMBO
Dad's telephone

COSTUME LIST

ACT I

BUDDY — T-shirt, trim fitting plaid undershorts (boxer), chinos or slacks, striped shirt (short-sleeve) tie, loafers, dark socks, socks with horses on them, second short-sleeve shirt, navy sportcoat, watch, wallet, change, briefcase, high school cardigan letter sweater

JENNY — Old robe, old unglamorous nightgown, slip, Laura Ashley dress, low heels, blue denim skirt, tailored shirt, flats, pearls, watch, earrings

DAD — Color shirt, tie, suit, sleeveless sweater

MIKE — Jeans, boots, plaid work shirt, slacks, sportshirt, loafers, measuring tape

MOM — Skirt, blouse, apron, low heels

BOOTS — Business suit, blouse, heels, briefcase and purse, skirt or dress with two jackets

ACT II

BUDDY — Slacks, sportshirt (short-sleeve), boxer shorts, loafers, socks, navy blue sportcoat, slacks, dress shirt (color), tie, seersucker or summer sportcoat, dress shirt, tie

JENNY — Bikini and pretty robe, nice summer dress, heels and purse, blue jeans and dressy sweater with price tag, formal black dress, lots of jewelry, dressy heels, 2 hair rollers, bra and halfslip

DAD — Dark suit, solid shirt, loose tie, slacks, shirtsleeves rolled up, raincoat, hat

MOM — Nice dress, heels, purse & sweater, casual skirt and blouse or sweatsuit, skirt and new blouse

MIKE — Slacks, sportcoat, tie, solid shirt, St. Louis Cardinals shirt or jacket, jeans, sneakers or loafers, boots, tuxedo, red rural handkerchief and bowtie

BOOTS — Three-quarter T shirt, sexy robe, pantsuit, boots, purse, jeans, sweatshirt, travel outfit, heels, briefcase, shoulder bag

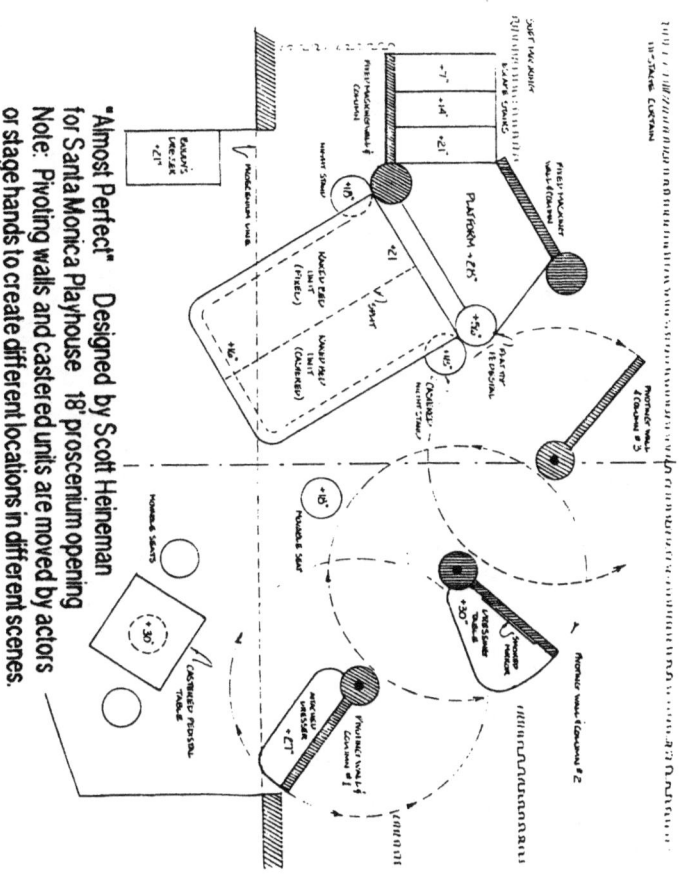

"Almost Perfect" Designed by Scott Heineman
for Santa Monica Playhouse 18' proscenium opening
Note: Pivoting walls and castered units are moved by actors
or stage hands to create different locations in different scenes.

www.ingramcontent.com/pod-product-compliance
Lightning Source LLC
Chambersburg PA
CBHW072014290426
44109CB00018B/2235